MEET ME IN THE
BAR

CLASSIC DRINKS FROM
AMERICA'S HISTORIC HOTELS

——

THOMAS CONNORS

PHOTOGRAPHY BY ERICKA McCONNELL
STYLED BY ALEXANDRA AND ELIOT ANGLE

STEWART, TABORI & CHANG
NEW YORK

Project editor: Sandra Gilbert
Production: Kim Tyner and Alexis Mentor

Published by
Stewart, Tabori & Chang
A Company of La Martinière Groupe
115 West 18th Street
New York, NY 10011

Export Sales to all countries except Canada,
France, and French-speaking Switzerland:
Thames and Hudson Ltd.
181A High Holborn
London WC1V 7QX
England

Canadian Distribution:
Canadian Manda Group
One Atlantic Avenue, Suite 105
Toronto, Ontario M6K 3E7
Canada

Library of Congress Cataloguing-in-Publication Data

Connors, Thomas (Thomas James)
Meet me in the bar : classic drinks from America's historic hotels / Thomas Connors;
drink photographs by Ericka McConnell.
p. cm.
ISBN 1-58479-293-0
1. Bars (Drinking establishment)—United States—Guidebook. 2. Cocktails.
3. Alcoholic beverages. I. Title.

TX950.56.C65 2003
647.9573—dc21   2003044920

The text of this book was composed in Sabon, Clarendon, and Interstate typefaces.

Design by Ivette Montes de Oca

Printed in Singapore

10 9 8 7 6 5 4 3 2 1
First Printing

ACKNOWLEDGMENTS

My many thanks to Sandy Gilbert for giving me the opportunity to write about one of my favorite subjects, to Sarah Scheffel, Jackie Kristel, and Elaine Schiebel for keeping me on track, and to my sister, Kate "She's Different" Lenn, research librarian extraordinaire.

———

For the weary business traveler, a bar stool and a beer are welcome relief. But when that drink is more than something to be thrown back with almost animal relief, when the sights and sounds around you are as much a part of the experience you're after as the glass in front of you, a proper hotel bar makes all the difference. And what makes for a proper hotel bar? A seriousness of purpose, a sense of style, and civility.

The thirty-six bars included here represent just some of the wonderful historic hotels around the country. The Peabody in Memphis, The Broadmoor in Colorado Springs, and the Clift in San Francisco, for example, are equally engaging. If you are lucky, there's at least one great hotel right in your own city. Cheers.

CONTENTS

PREFACE

There's nothing like the bar of a great hotel. I learned that on a business trip to Boston some years back. After dinner one evening, the convivial among us decided to have a nightcap. I can't remember where we'd eaten or how we all got from there to where we ended up—The Ritz-Carlton, Boston—but I will never forget walking into the Ritz bar for the first time. It was late, but the fireplace was still aglow and voices murmured from the darker corners of the room. The bartender, spruce in his crisp white jacket, discreetly acknowledged us with a nod of his head as he poured a drink for a gentleman at the bar. We settled in by the fire. And I haven't been the same since.

Although I still relish a visit to the corner tavern, increasingly, I find myself drawn to hotel bars, especially when traveling. A good bar in a fine hotel situates you in a strange city as firmly as any landmark. After all, the Oak Bar of The Plaza Hotel is as thoroughly New York as Central Park. The Top of the Mark signifies San Francisco as much as the Golden Gate Bridge. There's a sense of place to a great hotel bar, and though the city it manifests may not be my own, it is, somehow, for as long as I linger there. When peopled by local residents as well as out-of-towners, the bar of an established hotel exudes both the comfortable familiarity of a corner pub and the glamour and excitement peculiar to a room where people come and go, come and go.

I return to The Ritz-Carlton every time I visit Boston. I often land the same table, and on more than one occasion, the same waiter, who wonderfully enough, remembers me from my last visit. Stopping by recently, when the city was awash with recent graduates and their families, I watched as one happy group gathered there. A dapper young man looking somewhat abashed seemed to be the center of attention. Seated in the middle, he turned from left to right and back again as the conversation buzzed from one end of the table to the other. When they all rose to go, a little girl in the group skipped ahead, then turned and paused; her pale countenance shone against the room's dark wood like a face in a canvas by the great society painter, John Singer Sargent.

The fellow who'd steered us to The Ritz-Carlton that night years ago was a Boston-bred New Yorker, and for him, walking into that great hotel was as much a part of coming home as passing through the door of the house he was raised in. I can't lay claim to the city in the same way, but in the bar of the Ritz, I'm sure I feel as much at home in Boston as that old Brahmin.

MEET ME IN THE

BAR

ONLY A FEW OF THE OLD-TIME HOTELS ARE HOLDING OUT AGAINST THE ENCROACHMENTS OF TIME AND THE ONSLAUGHTS OF COMPETITION. –JEFFERSON WILLIAMSON, *THE AMERICAN HOTEL*

When Mr. Williamson made that mournful observation in 1930, his lament was for mid-nineteenth-century hotels, establishments that were not always that far removed from the rustic inns and rough city taverns that preceded them. When the Gilsey House opened in New York in 1871, the inaugural celebration was so spirited that the place had to be closed the next day for repairs. No doubt, alcohol had something to do with it.

Liquor and lodging have been partners from the start. In early America, when ale and rum were drunk more than water, a tavern was often more than just a taproom; spotting its swinging shingle, a weary traveler knew he had found a place to spend the night. Or course, the bed he climbed into was not necessarily his alone–sharing with strangers was commonplace–but with a tasty draught and a place to lay his head, he was well taken care of.

As early as 1794, hotels began to supplant the humble tavern in New York, Boston, and Philadelphia. By the 1840s, New Orleans and St. Louis boasted superior accommodations, too, and with the growth of the railroad, any city that thought much of itself soon erected at least one big hotel. The tavern-as-inn was on its way out, but the bar that had been such a key component of those early inns did not disappear. In *A Diary of America, with Remarks on its Institutions* (1839), English writer Frederick Marryat noted, "the recreations of most Americans are politics and news, besides the chance of doing a little more business, all of which, with drink, are to be obtained at the bars of the principal commercial hotels . . . "

MARLENE DIETRICH AT THE BEVERLY HILLS HOTEL

INTRODUCTION

* * *

After visiting the barroom at Boston's Tremont House on his first tour of North America in 1842, Charles Dickens wrote "there . . . the stranger is initiated into the mysteries of the Sherry cobbler, Sangaree, Timber Doodle, and other rare drinks." Twelve years later, the Parker House opened, and soon Boston businessmen were wheeling and dealing in its bar. And they weren't the only ones. So diligently did local collegians recreate there that humorist Artemus Ward was led to remark, "Harvard University was pleasantly and conveniently situated in the barroom of Parker's in School Street."

Reporting on the Civil War for *The Atlantic Monthly*, Nathaniel Hawthorne was put up at the antecedent of today's Willard Hotel, where, he observed, "you adopt the universal habit of place, and call for a mint julep, a whisky-skin, a gin-cocktail, a brandy-smash or a glass of pure Old Rye, for the conviviality of Washington sets in at an early hour, and, so far as I had an opportunity of observing, never terminates at any hour, and all those drinks are continually in request by almost all these people."

As hotels grew larger and more architecturally elaborate, the bars went from a plank laid over a couple of barrels to beautifully crafted pieces of furniture set in their own richly appointed rooms. Manhattan's Hoffman House, erected in 1864 and closed in 1915, was outfitted with paintings by the sixteenth-century Italian master Correggio and the then contemporary Frenchman, Adolphe-William Bouguereau. Maxfield Parrish's mural *Old King Cole*, now in New York's St. Regis, hung in the bar of the Knickerbocker Hotel at Broadway and 42nd Street before that 1906 property went the way of the wrecking ball in 1920.

The cocktail, the name Americans have used for certain mixed drinks since at least 1806, coursed to ever-greater popularity in these upscale surroundings. The Rickey was reportedly invented in the 1870s at the bar of New York's St. James Hotel when one guest, a Colonel Rickey of Callaway County, Missouri, produced some limes and asked the barman to concoct a drink around them. Bartender Jerry Thomas, a fixture at the Occidental Hotel in San Francisco, the Metropolitan in New York, and the Planters's Hotel in St. Louis (where he invented the Tom and Jerry), compiled dozens of recipes in *The Bon Vivant's Companion or How to Mix Drinks* (1862). His concoctions ranged from the elaborate to the formidably simple; the Spread Eagle Punch called for one bottle of scotch, one bottle of rye, sugar, lemon peel, and boiling water "at discretion." A man who considered imbibing a gentlemanly art, Thomas—who went by the moniker "Professor"—was quick to promote the limits of indulgence. His nonrecipe for a shot of brandy warned, "In serving this drink you simply put a piece of ice in a tumbler and hand to your customer, with the bottle of brandy. This is very safe for a steady drink, but though a *straight* beverage, it is often used on a *bender*."

The nation's early temperance movements had little impact on hotel bars; if anything, the growing disapprobation simply encouraged drinkers to forsake the dining room for the bar, where they could lift a glass in relative privacy. But the Volstead Act finally did its damage. Corks ceased to pop, glasses no longer clinked. The Oak Bar at New York's Plaza Hotel became an office of E. F. Hutton; the bar at the Hotel Jerome in Aspen was turned into a soda fountain. What Prohibition failed to stifle, the Depression did. The Beverly Hills Hotel was just one of many hotels forced to close its doors.

Even those properties that survived did not emerge unscathed. In the decades that followed, the general democratization of travel (propelled by the interstate highway system and its attendant motels) and the hospitality industry's consequent cutbacks in services and style greatly diminished many hotels. The Willard in Washington faltered in the 1940s, closed in 1968, and did not reopen until 1986. In the 1970s, the marble floors of Boston's Copley Plaza were covered with cheap tile and a garish neon sign was stuck on her roof. The latter may have been fine for Times Square, but it didn't go over well in Back Bay. Worst of all, many great barrooms were converted to other uses, or cruelly refashioned so that they possessed about as much spirit as an airport cocktail lounge.

Luckily, in recent years, a number of America's great old hotels have been acquired by first-rate chains and other sensitive operators whose multimillion-dollar renovations and increased attention to service have restored them to their former magnificence. Although luxurious hotels continue to be built, the great city hotels of the past—marble palaces with richly ornamented lobbies, dining rooms that make one want to sit up straight, and *proper* bars—remain in a class by themselves.

THE HOTELS

THE NORTHEAST

MASSACHUSETTS **BOSTON** THE FAIRMONT COPLEY PLAZA THE RITZ-CARLTON, BOSTON	**15**
NEW YORK **NEW YORK CITY** THE ALGONQUIN HOTEL THE CARLYLE THE PLAZA HOTEL THE ST. REGIS HOTEL	**20**

THE FAIRMONT COPLEY PLAZA

The Fairmont Copley Plaza sits on one of Boston's great public spaces, Copley Square, where its companions include H. H. Richardson's Romanesque Trinity Church; McKim, Mead and White's Italianate Boston Public Library; and one of the first buildings to give the city a twentieth-century skyline, I. M. Pei's wedge-shaped John Hancock Tower. The hotel opened in 1912 with both Mayor John F. Fitzgerald (grandfather of the president) and President Howard Taft in attendance.

Compared to the living room-like intimacy of the bar at The Ritz-Carlton, the Copley bar is enormous. For years, it was known as the Merry-Go-Round Bar and sported a carousel where one could sit and slowly spin while enjoying a drink. Peggy Dray, the hotel's director of special events and community affairs, grew up in the area and remembers those days well. "Back in the late fifties, when my husband and I were both in college, the Merry-Go-Round Bar was very much a part of everyone's life in Boston. We'd meet there after the men had played squash, or end an evening there after being out elsewhere. It was warm and friendly, you'd see your contemporaries there, and as we became young married couples, it remained a very special place to go on a special occasion."

For Bostonians of a younger generation, the bar will always be the Oak Bar, the name it assumed in the 1970s. It was then that the carousel made its final revolution and the room was refashioned in the manner of a British officer's club, complete with canvas ceiling fans. Swagged, gold drapes now adorn the large windows; lamps sit on pedestals arranged throughout the room, offering the dimmest light from under softly hued shades. Dark wood paneling adds to the dusky ambiance.

When the Copley Plaza opened ninety-one years ago, one reporter remarked, "Boston people take a personal interest in their hotels and support them loyally." Sitting beneath the Oak Bar's great coffered ceiling today, it's easy to see that they still do. Ladies of a certain age (in sensible wool suits), elderly gents sitting eminently erect, and blue-blazered youths and their girlfriends all transmit an almost possessive air as they make their way to their favorite table or cuddle up at the bar. "There are people," suggests Dray, "for whom the Copley Plaza and the Oak Bar will always mean something special. It's a place they've gone through a lifetime with, as I have."

THE FAIRMONT COPLEY PLAZA
138 ST. JAMES AVENUE
BOSTON, MASSACHUSETTS
617.267.5300

THE ICE BLUE MARTINI (SIGNATURE DRINK)
DRINK RECIPE 1

OAK BAR SIDECAR
DRINK RECIPE 2

THE BERRIES
DRINK RECIPE 3

THE OAK BAR (LEFT) AND OAK ROOM RESTAURANT (ABOVE) ARE THE HEART AND SOUL OF THE FAIRMONT COPLEY PLAZA.

THE RITZ-CARLTON, BOSTON

The Ritz-Carlton, Boston opened in 1927. In those less-hurried days, its amenities included perfumed elevators, ice skates for a spin on the Public Garden's pond, wood-burning fireplaces (still intact in the hotel's suites), and twenty-four-hour room service, a rarity back then. Alas, debuting as it did during Prohibition, the hotel did not feature a bar. That shortcoming was corrected at the first possible opportunity—in 1933, to be exact.

Edward Wyner, who owned and ran the hotel at that time, was a Harvard man, Class of 1918. That pedigree, and the proximity of the university, made the bar a popular haunt for the boys from Cambridge. So popular, in fact, that in 1948, Wyner felt compelled to issue guidelines to his staff to keep the crew from across the Charles from overrunning The Ritz-Carlton. Wyner prescribed that a man not only had to be 21, but to look it, lest other guests suspect the management of corrupting youth. A baby-faced boy was simply out of luck. "We do not want to be criticized," he noted, "so this poor young man cannot be served. Maybe he will never look over 21 and this poor young man will go through life without ever getting a drink at the Ritz Bar."

As for attire, Wyner stated, "We do not want young men, even when they are obviously over 21 and eligible to be served . . . who are not properly dressed. Not properly dressed means the college boy uniform of odd coat and pants. Odd coat means a coat not part of a regular suit. It usually comes in bright patterns and is very appropriate dress for college wear. It is not,

however, the proper dress to patronize the Ritz Bar."

Although the bar continues to draw customers from Harvard—after all, the university and the hotel share a social milieu—no one would describe a descent down the marble entry steps as crucial to a young woman's future. But in an unenlightened era not so long past, many assumed that the bar, crowded with bright college boys, afforded many a "girl" a first glimpse of her future husband.

Back in the days when Broadway producers routinely opened a show in Boston before taking it to New York, theater folk often stopped at The Ritz-Carlton and many, no doubt, visited the bar. Moss Hart, whose *Light Up the Sky* is set in The Ritz-Carlton said, "One of the reasons I try to open shows in Boston is so that I can stay at the hotel." Oscar Hammerstein composed the "Edelweiss" number for *The Sound of Music* here, Tennessee Williams tweaked *A Streetcar Named Desire* in his room, and Neil Simon penned the third act of *The Odd Couple* after checking in.

With its armchairs and sofas, fireplace and view of the Public Garden, the walnut-paneled Ritz-Carlton Bar remains an incomparably comfortable place to relax—whatever your alma mater or creative bent.

THE RITZ-CARLTON, BOSTON
15 ARLINGTON STREET
BOSTON, MASSACHUSETTS
617.536.5700

THE BOSTON RITZ FIZZ (SIGNATURE DRINK)
DRINK RECIPE 4

THE ALGONQUIN HOTEL

The charm of The Algonquin Hotel endures *despite* a fabled history. Home of the renowned Round Table of wits and birthplace of *The New Yorker*, The Algonquin is so closely identified with American literary life between the wars that it could well have become a relic, or worse, a shrine. But aside from an unnecessary nod or two to its past—such as renaming the Rose Room dining room The Round Table Room—The Algonquin is quite simply a small hotel whose public spaces recall another era. (Of course, if it weren't for its literary connections, the hotel could well have been razed, or at the very least, modishly redone as a trendy boutique establishment.)

That voluble gathering known as the Round Table, came about in 1919 when press agent John Peter Toohey threw a party for critic Alexander Woollcott, who was returning to *The New York Times* after wartime duty as a writer for *Stars & Stripes.* But Toohey had a beef with Woollcott. He'd asked him to plug Eugene O'Neill in the *Times* and when Woollcott refused, Toohey deliberately misspelled the writer's name on the party invitations. But Woollcott didn't take offense and the bash was such a success, Toohey himself said, "Why don't we do this every day?"

For ten years, Woollcott and his crowd— Dorothy Parker, George F. Kaufman, Franklin P. Adams, Edna Ferber, Marc Connelly, Robert Sherwood, and Robert Benchley—did just that. Their repartee, real and imagined, became the stuff of legend. They met for lunch in what was then called the Pergola Room, later christened the Oak Room. Owner Frank Case, always partial to actors and scribes, appreciated the growing renown of this midday pack and set them up at a round table in the more visible Rose Room, situated right off the lobby. As for *The New Yorker*, the magazine got its start upstairs when its founder Harold Ross put the bite on fellow poker player and yeast heir Raoul Fleishmann for a loan of $25,000.

Although The Algonquin has a separate bar, the pubby and masculine Blue Bar (and at one time, another tiny one tucked away near the front door), the lobby itself functions as a bar. So much so that it's difficult to think of the lobby as anything other than a bar. The little bellman bells set on each table ding with the regularity of an old clock as patrons summon one of the dark-suited waiters who are always weaving through the room, ever ready to take an order.

Anyone who hasn't visited the hotel in some time might be dismayed that the carpet and upholstery are in better repair than they remember (genteel shabbiness was once a point of pride here). The little news-

THE ALGONQUIN HOTEL
59 WEST 44TH STREET
NEW YORK, NEW YORK
212.840.6800

MATILDA
DRINK RECIPE 5

VICIOUS CIRCLE
DRINK RECIPE 6

stand that hugged one corner of the lobby was removed back in the eighties, and the old accordion-door phone booth by the elevator is gone too, but the essence of the lobby remains unchanged. Oak-paneled piers still break up the space like so many trees (one always has to poke about to find one's party), the less-than-luxuriant potted palms linger on, and the sofas are as soft as ever. As always, a sense of purposeful coming and going pervades. New Yorkers rush in with a proprietary air, out-of-towners advance with a curiosity that borders on reverence, and everyone, it seems, departs well comforted.

THE CARLYLE

New York is ever-changing. Districts that were once dead after dark are now abuzz with activity. Buildings never meant for human habitation have been retrofitted as fancy private residences. Neighborhoods abandoned as families moved up and out, are being reclaimed by a new generation. But Manhattan's Upper East Side, from Fifth to Park Avenues, remains essentially unchanged. Packed with more money, power, and prestige than almost any residential district in the country (some would say the world), it is the cynosure of all that is chic and costly. True, not everyone wants to live here, not even those who could easily afford to do so—it's just too *too*. And to the more democratically minded or adventurous, it's too much of too little. But for countless dreamers, the idea of it is just delectable.

Located on the corner of 76th Street at Madison Avenue, The Carlyle stands at the epicenter of this heady world. The hotel went up in 1930, the brainchild of the ambitious developer Moses Ginsburg. For years, it was run like a private club; social references were de rigueur for anyone seeking accommodation. And what accommodation. Its various owners have always relied on top interior designers—Dorothy Draper, Mark Hampton, Thierry Despont—to provide guests and residents with the most tasteful surroundings.

In 1947, Ludwig Bemelmans, an artist whose work appeared in *The New Yorker* and *Town & Country*, was engaged to paint murals in what was then known simply as the hotel bar. An Austrian émigré who had worked in hotels and restaurants on both sides of the Atlantic, Bemelmans landed Stateside in 1914 in a bid to avoid reform school for reportedly having shot a waiter. Although he authored a number of novels and essays, Bemelmans is perhaps best known for his wildly popular children's book *Madeline* and its well-loved successors. For all the sweet fancy of his stories and illustrations, Bemelmans was one sharp negotiator; payment for the Carlyle murals included 18 months' lodging for his family.

THE CARLYLE
MADISON AVENUE AT 76TH STREET
NEW YORK, NEW YORK
212.744.1600

THE OLD CUBAN
DRINK RECIPE 7

DESIGN IS KING AT THE CARLYLE, FROM THE COZY NOOKS IN BEMELMANS (ABOVE) TO THE RESTRAINED ELEGANCE OF THE LOBBIES.

Bemelmans is a thrillingly intimate space, combining the away-from-it-all romance of a little *cave* in Paris, the suave appointments of a club car in the glory days of rail travel, and the relaxed yet sophisticated atmosphere of a den in an elegant town house. Recently refreshed with a gold-leaf ceiling and lampshades made to match Bemelmans' whimsical take on Central Park (where sophisticated rabbits dine under an umbrella), Bemelmans Bar is quite simply *sui generis*. Step into it and you feel as if you've been admitted, without embarrassing fanfare, to some very private club. Whether relaxing within its cocoonlike afternoon stillness, or enjoying the jazz combo that draws a crowd in the evening, you won't believe your good fortune.

THE PLAZA HOTEL

No tour of America's historic hotels would be complete without The Plaza. It's not the oldest hotel we will visit. It's not even the most glamorous or exclusive property in New York. (To my mind, the St. Regis holds the first title, and The Carlyle the second.) But no hotel has succeeded in capturing the public's imagination quite like The Plaza. It has done so since October 1, 1907, when Mr. and Mrs. Alfred Vanderbilt were the first to sign its register.

The Plaza has always enjoyed the patronage of high society and the celebrated. In Edwardian days, some of the country's most illustriously wealthy families were permanent residents; in the 1920s, Scott and Zelda flapped away upstairs and down. Truman Capote threw his legendary Black and White Ball for *Washington Post* publisher Katherine Graham there in 1966. Ivana Trump ran the hotel in the 1980s, and most recently, The Plaza was the locus of a media frenzy when actors Michael Douglas and Catherine Zeta-Jones were wed on the premises.

Yet, for all the bold-face names, The Plaza was built in the democratic spirit that characterized the American hotel from the start, the belief that a great hotel could be as civic a building as City Hall or the public library. So it remains. The rich and famous might parade proprietarily through it, but one needn't check in to check it out. Enter The Plaza today and you'll spot CEOs, stars, and out-of-towners determined to experience New York at its best. But you will also encounter everyday New Yorkers at tea, or a mother from almost anywhere taking her daughter to see where Eloise, the heroine of Kay Thompson's children's books, had so much naughty fun.

Situated on Fifth Avenue and 59th Street overlooking Central Park, The Plaza is quite simply one of the most visible buildings in Manhattan. At age ninety-six, it seems to have been there forever. But, in fact, this is the second Plaza Hotel to occupy the site. The first, built in the 1880s and a very impressive property in its day, came down in 1905 when Harry St. Francis Black, president of the Fuller Construction Company, acquired the property. He, along with Bernard Beinecke, a wholesale-meat merchant and owner of several other hotels in the city, and Fred Sterry, who managed such distinguished properties as the Breakers in Palm Beach, gathered investors to replace the existing hotel with an even finer property. To achieve their goal, this troika engaged Henry Janeway Hardenbergh, the New Jersey-born architect whose past projects included the first Waldorf-Astoria Hotel and Washington's Hotel Willard, as well as the imposing Dakota Apartments across Central Park. Hardenbergh created an edifice whose lines recall French châteaux and whose interiors offered New Yorkers some of the most sumptuous public spaces in the city. The central Palm Court is clearly one such space, but the room that really captures the energy and attitude of the city is the Oak Bar.

A big room with a long bar and paneling so dark it's almost black, the Oak Bar is impressive but not overly elegant. It is in fact a glorified saloon, as hotel bars were early on, and this accounts for much of its appeal. Murals of old New York, installed in the 1940s when Conrad Hilton owned the hotel, adorn the walls and four huge windows offer a view of Central Park across the street.

It's a bit disconcerting to see sneakers and jeans in the Oak Bar these days, but this disappointment is offset by the attentions of a mature staff, all of whom treat their jobs as careers, not way stations to stardom. Bartender Orlando Rivera has been with The Plaza for fifteen years. In that time, he has served his share of moguls and movie actors. But when asked to recall a particularly memorable evening in the Oak Bar, the night he describes—Christmas Eve, 2002—has nothing to do with the powerful or famous. "It was snowing and the bar was packed. You'd be surprised. A lot of people want to sit in the Oak Bar and look out at Central Park in the snow. To me, that was a magic moment."

THE PLAZA HOTEL
FIFTH AVENUE AT 59TH STREET
NEW YORK, NEW YORK
212.759.3000

OLD FASHIONED
DRINK RECIPE 8

LONG ISLAND ICED TEA
DRINK RECIPE 9

BRONX COCKTAIL
DRINK RECIPE 10

THE ST. REGIS HOTEL

As America's inns grew from simple houses to skyscraping heights, many enterprising hoteliers sought to conjure the kind of opulence only a robber baron could normally enjoy. But New York's St. Regis was built by John Jacob Astor IV, a man whose family virtually wrote the book on the good life. The Colonel, as he was known, was the son of *the* Mrs. Astor, the social lioness who admitted only the highest of high society to her Fifth Avenue mansion.

Hotels were in his blood. His great-grandfather, John Jacob Astor, founder of the family fortune, built Astor House (one of the greatest hotels of its day) in lower Manhattan in the 1830s. And John Jacob IV had already joined forces with his cousin William Waldorf Astor to build the first Waldorf-Astoria—where the Empire State Building now stands.

The St. Regis played a key role in transforming Fifth Avenue from a street of mansions to a thoroughfare of hotels and carriage trade retailers. When the Colonel built it in 1904, he spared no expense, opting for marble floors and crystal chandeliers, antique tapestries, Louis XV furniture, and a 3,000-volume library with its own librarian at his guests' disposal. At one time or another, the St. Regis has been home to CBS president Bill Paley and his wife, Babe, actress Marlene Dietrich, and the surrealist Salvador Dali. And with its astoundingly attentive staff and beautifully maintained premises, it remains one of the city's most imposingly elegant hotels.

For all its gilt and marble, the pride of the hotel's public spaces is the dark, wood-paneled King Cole Bar, home of Maxfield Parrish's large mural, *Old King Cole.* The twenty-eight-foot work shows the King with a fatuous grimace on his face, sheepish in spectacles and a crown that looks as much a party favor as it does truly regal headgear. His Fiddler's Three attend him with a knowing haughtiness.

This wasn't the first time Parrish, the immensely popular painter and illustrator, tackled this subject; in 1894, the Mask and Wig Club at the University of Pennsylvania hired him to decorate its premises along the same theme. Astor had commissioned the *Old King Cole* mural for his Knickerbocker Hotel at Broadway and 42nd Street in 1906. After that property was razed in 1920, the mural hung for a time in the Art Institute of Chicago and later in the New York Racquet and Tennis Club.

Like the painting, the bar itself hasn't sat still. For years, it was located along the Fifth Avenue side of the hotel in a space formerly known as the Iridium Room, a popular nightclub with a skating rink beneath its floor. That room was renamed the King Cole Grille in 1948 and Parrish's picture—big, bright, and storybook appealing—was hung over the bar. In 1991, both the

THE ST. REGIS HOTEL
2 EAST 55TH STREET AT FIFTH AVENUE
NEW YORK, NEW YORK
212.753.4500

THE RED SNAPPER
DRINK RECIPE 11

bar and the painting traveled west, past the lobby and the airy Astor Court to the present space.

The Bloody Mary—made famous at Harry's New York Bar in Paris during the Roaring Twenties—arrived in New York City courtesy of St. Regis bartender Fernand Petiot. Petiot, who had poured the vodka-based libation himself in Paris, enhanced it stateside with the addition of salt, pepper, lemon, and Worcestershire sauce. The name Bloody Mary struck someone at the St. Regis as a tad too rough, so the drink was renamed the Red Snapper. People order a lot of Bloody Marys at the St. Regis, according to veteran barman Jim Higgins. But the drink is still listed on the menu as the Red Snapper.

THE WARMLY LIT ST. REGIS GLOWS LIKE A JEWEL AT DUSK (LEFT). MAXFIELD PARRISH'S OLD KING COLE (RIGHT) MAKES THE HOTEL'S BAR ONE OF THE MOST COLORFUL ROOMS IN THE CITY.

THE PARK HYATT PHILADELPHIA
AT THE BELLEVUE

What's in a name? Plenty. A name on the tongue is what a physical presence is to the eye—the thing itself. Yet what happens when a name changes but the place it signifies remains essentially the same? While even the oldest old-timer in New York would never refer to JFK airport by its original name, Idlewild, you still find some not so old-timers who call the Met Life Building the Pan Am Building—its name when the building first hit the skyline. And while the San Francisco 49ers now play in 3-Com Park, you'd be hard-pressed to find a local who doesn't still refer to the team's home as Candlestick Park.

Speaking of names, the Park Hyatt Philadelphia at the Bellevue is quite a mouthful. But unlike The Plaza Hotel in New York, which has always been The Plaza, the Park Hyatt is a tenant in the Bellevue, a mixed-use building that was initially erected as a hotel. Older Philadelphians and long-time visitors to the city have known the property by various names over the years, the Bellevue-Stratford Hotel, the Fairmont, and Hotel Atop the Bellevue. Today, it's commonly, and more simply, referred to as the Park Hyatt or the Bellevue.

A French Renaissance-style edifice, the property opened as the Bellevue-Stratford Hotel in 1904. It was the creation of George C. Boldt, a Prussian immigrant who after acquiring two small hotel properties on Philadelphia's Broad Street, the Stratford and the Bellevue, broke ground on his 1,000-room Bellevue-Stratford in 1902. It was run by a staff of seven hundred, a workforce that included a brigade of women whose sole responsibility was to pack the trunks of female guests.

The hotel quickly became a magnet for the city's elite. In 1909, citizens honoring impresario Oscar Hammerstein, who built the Philadelphia Opera House, sat down to a multi-course meal accompanied by Sauternes, sherry, and champagne. The menu, written in French (except for the first course—grapefruit), was illustrated with musical motifs and heraldic wreathes. And generations of Philadelphians have descended the grand staircase of the hotel's ballroom—illuminated by fixtures designed by Thomas Alva Edison—to enjoy one gala after another.

These days, as hotel operators jazz up old properties for a younger clientele, it's possible to walk into a sober-looking hotel and discover that that sensible bar you once knew is now a scene. Luckily, the 19th-floor Library Lounge at the Park Hyatt is nothing like that. This gracious room is a very civilized retreat, as

THE PARK HYATT PHILADELPHIA AT THE BELLEVUE
BROAD AND WALNUT STREETS
PHILADELPHIA, PENNSYLVANIA
215.893.1776

THE CLOVER CLUB
DRINK RECIPE 12

popular with the scions of Philadelphia society as it is with visiting CEOs.

A small space seating about thirty-five, the bar, with its rich woodwork, fireplace, and books—all related in some way to Philadelphia—conjures the library of a grand private residence. Popular today with theatergoers before and after a show and as a meeting place for hotel guests as they head out to dinner, the bar proudly serves The Clover Club, arguably the spirituous equivalent of the famous Philly cheese steak. According to Albert Stevens Crockett, author of *Old Waldorf Bar Days* (1931), the Clover Club cocktail—gin with an egg white, lime, raspberry syrup, and bitters—"originated, it is said, in the bar of the old Bellevue-Stratford, where the Clover Club, composed of literary, legal, financial, and business lights of the Quaker City, often dined and wined and wined again."

A GENTLEMAN ALWAYS FEELS RIGHT AT HOME IN THE LIBRARY LOUNGE OF THE PARK HYATT AT THE BELLEVUE. BUILT AS THE BELLEVUE-STRATFORD (RIGHT), THE HOTEL SITS IN THE HEART OF PHILADELPHIA.

THE MID-CENTURY CHIC OF THE CONTINENTAL AND SOME OF THE STYLISH MEN WHO MET THERE.

OMNI WILLIAM PENN HOTEL

America's robber barons weren't out to be loved. But they sure put on a good show. While alive or after they were gone, Carnegie and Rockefeller and their kind threw their millions to all sorts of good causes, from universities and libraries to museums and hospitals. Pittsburgh's own titan, the coke and steel magnate Henry Clay Frick, was no friend to labor or much of anyone else, and for decades his industries soiled Pittsburgh unmercifully. But ultimately, his sense of noblesse oblige led him to create parkland, support medical centers, and assist a number of local philanthropic organizations. And before he died in 1919, Frick gave the city a little something else to remember him by: the William Penn Hotel.

Named after the founder of the Pennsylvania colony, the hotel opened in 1916. From the start, it was the place for the city's movers and shakers to meet and greet. Unlike other hotels of the era, which were erected to serve a decidedly upscale clientele, some of whom lived in these properties full-time, the William Penn's location in industrial Pittsburgh meant it had to cater more to businessmen and the convention crowd. Which isn't to suggest that Frick scrimped on elegance. Walnut and green marble graced the lobby, gold leaf and chandeliers adorned the ballroom, bucolic murals ran along the corridors, and the guestrooms were furnished with reproduction antiques.

The hotel's sumptuousness was such that in 1937 one publication proclaimed, "Surrounded by all the luxuries that human ingenuity and expenditure can produce . . . so provided for is the guest that he might inhabit the hotel's corridors for years without venturing out into the harsh realities of sunlight."

For the cocktail fancier, that included seven bars, a situation hard to imagine today at all but the most sprawling resorts (or a Vegas casino). The Continental, arguably the hotel's premier barroom, opened in 1934. This "repealorium," as the hotel manager's cleverly called it, was an Art Deco chamber with a ceiling done in blue, gold, and silver; a canvas by local artist Malcolm Parcell, *The Judgment of Paris*, hung behind the bar. In 1958, the room was redone and named Sign of the Harp & Crown, after what had been the city's leading tavern in 1796. It was renamed the Tap Room in 1984 and so it remains today.

OMNI WILLIAM PENN HOTEL
530 WILLIAM PENN PLACE
PITTSBURGH, PENNSYLVANIA
412.281.7100

CONTINENTAL BAR MANHATTAN
DRINK RECIPE 13

RENAISSANCE MAYFLOWER HOTEL

Designed by local architect Robert F. Beresford and by Whitney Warren and Charles Wetmore, the New York–based team behind Grand Central Terminal and such hotels as the Broadmoor in Colorado Springs, the Mayflower has been greatly admired for its style and service. President Harry Truman, who lived at the hotel for his first ninety days in office, called it the "second best address in Washington." Built in 1925, the Mayflower continues to make a good impression, drawing a high-profile clientele from the worlds of politics, media, business, and the arts.

Opening as it did during Prohibition, the Mayflower came into the world dry. But it lost its innocence when it played host to both those who crusaded for a saner republic and those who saw gin and thought sin. Already a meeting place for the Women's Organization for National Prohibition Reform, in March 1931, the hotel hosted a gathering of the Democratic National Committee, at which both committee chairman John J. Raskob and presidential nominee Alfred E. Smith raised the issue of repeal over a national radio broadcast. Eight months later, the Mayflower welcomed the Woman's Christian Temperance Union, and in 1932, the Anti-Saloon League of America.

After Repeal was enacted in December 1933, the hotel quickly acquired a liquor license (the first in the District of Columbia) and opened the Mayflower Men's Bar in 1934. The hotel billed the bar as "an entirely new room with the atmosphere of a private club." Its advertisements also noted, "Patronage Restricted To MEN." Ladies wishing something more exciting than tea could take it in the Mayflower Lounge, the post-Prohibition name for the area formerly known as the Palm Court.

In time, the Men's Bar became known as the Town & Country Lounge, where the sexes have mingled quite happily for decades. The room's continuing popularity can be attributed in part to the man behind the bar, Sambonn Lek. Dubbed the "Alan Greenspan of the capital's bar scene" by the *Washington Post*, Lek has been with the Mayflower for twenty-seven years. When he's not shaking up one of the various martinis he's concocted, he's liable to divert customers with his repertoire of card tricks or by levitating $20 bills. (Lek insists lesser denominations just won't float.)

RENAISSANCE MAYFLOWER HOTEL
1127 CONNECTICUT AVENUE, NW
WASHINGTON, D.C.
202.347.3000

MAYFLOWER ROYAL (SIGNATURE DRINK)
DRINK RECIPE 14

TOWN & COUNTRY (SIGNATURE DRINK)
DRINK RECIPE 15

STEPS FROM THE WILLARD'S SOARING LOBBY SITS THE SNUG ROUND ROBIN BAR.

THE WILLARD INTER-CONTINENTAL WASHINGTON

F. Scott Fitzgerald's aphorism, "There are no second acts in American life," is a great quote because it backfires so beautifully. After all, reinvention is our national M.O., and as much as we love to see the mighty fall, we love it even more when they rise again. But are there third acts? When it comes to hotels, the Willard certainly enjoys that distinction.

The first Willard opened in 1850, when Henry Willard and his brother Edwin (former bartenders on Hudson River steamboats) bought Fuller's City Hotel and renamed it Willard's City Hotel. In 1901, Henry's nephew Joseph expanded the property, creating one of the capital's first skyscrapers, a Beaux Arts structure by Henry Janeway Hardenbergh, who later designed Boston's Copley Plaza and The Plaza Hotel in New York. Forty-five years later, the Willard's glory days were over: Pennsylvania Avenue was looking less than stately and the Willard family sold the property in 1946. It continued on as a hotel, but went down with the neighborhood. Shuttered in 1968, it didn't reopen until 1986.

Today, the Willard is once again one of Washington's premier hotels, and its Round Robin Bar is a destination for both Washingtonians and all those who seem to come and go so quickly here. Just like the old Willard bar. Exhorting Union troops, Walt Whitman exclaimed, "Where are your men? . . . Sneak, blow, put on airs there in Willard's sumptuous . . . barrooms . . . no explanation will save you. Bull Run is your work . . . " In 1904, Round Robin regulars waged a war of their own. As temperance leader Carrie Nation went swinging her intemperate hatchet, a sign was posted in the Round Robin Bar proclaiming, "All Nations Welcome Except Carrie."

Although the original circular bar was ripped out years ago, an admirable successor now anchors the room, allowing patrons to jump in and out of conversations as easily as ever. But few politicians imbibe as openly as they once did. "If I got a nickel for every glass of soda water I served in a wineglass to a senator or congressman," notes bartender Jim Hewes, "I'd be a wealthy man."

Located within blocks of the White House and the Capitol Building, the Willard and its bar are ideally positioned to capture Washington's unique energy. Lobbyists and politicians, lawyers and CEOs, movers and those just hoping to shake things up pass in and out of the Round Robin. "You can walk in and find yourself sitting next to Gore Vidal," suggests Hewes, "and then in walks some attorney who was on *Larry King* last night. It's like Wednesdays at the Mickey Mouse Club—Anything Can Happen Day."

THE WILLARD INTER-CONTINENTAL WASHINGTON
1401 PENNSYLVANIA AVENUE, NW
WASHINGTON, D.C.
202.628.9100

HENRY CLAY'S SOUTHERN-STYLE MINT JULEP
(SIGNATURE DRINK)
DRINK RECIPE 16

THE GREENBRIER

Folks have been coming to this neck of the woods for a long, long time. The Shawnee were the first to sample the springs here; the first white person reported to have enjoyed their salutary effect was a rheumatic woman who arrived on a litter in 1778. It's said she walked home. Soon others came, pitching tents and their hopes on a cure. Before long, simple cottages sprung up.

Although this rural retreat was tough to get to and was a far cry from the luxurious spa it would become (one visitor described it as "decidedly the meanest, most nasty place in point of filth, dust and every other bad quality"), the putatively healthful properties of its water were a powerful draw. According to one 1834 visitor, the spring was believed to be good for whatever ailed you: "Yellow Jaundice, White Swelling, Blue Devils, and Black Plague, Scarlet Fever, Yellow Fever, Spotted Fever, and fever of every kind and color . . . Dispepsia, Diarrhea, Diabetes, and die of anything; Gout, Gourmandising, and Grogging . . . and all other diseases and bad habits, except chewing, smoking, spitting, and swearing." But even then, not every visitor was driven hither in the name of good health. As the fellow above drolly noted, in addition to the mineral content of the waters, "fashion" was key to the appeal of White Sulphur Springs and "no doubt contributes greatly to the efficiency of the water."

His observation proved spot on. As years passed, White Sulphur Springs became yet another stylish destination for America's ruling class who wintered here or summered there. The Astors, Armours, Dukes, Drexels, Vanderbilts, and Biddles all returned again and again for the pampering and socializing.

The first large inn to serve this elite crowd opened in 1858. Guests had long referred to the White Sulphur Springs resort simply as the White and they did the same with the new hotel. As the hotel aged, it became known as the Old White. Four hundred feet long and four stories tall, with Doric columns and a dining room which seated twelve hundred, the Old White survived the Civil War (a Union general was dissuaded from burning it down) and remained in service until 1922, when it failed to pass the fire code. But by then, the first phase of today's Greenbrier had already been erected and the resort was able to operate without interruption.

Like the Old White, which was shuttered during the Civil War, the Greenbrier was off limits to civilians during World War II. At first, the property was used as an internment camp for German and Japanese diplo-

THE GREENBRIER
300 WEST MAIN STREET
WHITE SULPHUR SPRINGS, WEST VIRGINIA
304.536.1110

THE SCARLETT O'HARA (SIGNATURE DRINK)
DRINK RECIPE 17

THE RHODODENDRON (SIGNATURE DRINK)
DRINK RECIPE 18

mats, and later, as a military hospital. When the hotel resumed business in 1948, the guest list for its reopening party included Harry and Bess Truman, the Duke and Duchess of Windsor, Bing Crosby, Fred Astaire, and a thirty-one-year-old congressman named John Fitzgerald Kennedy.

Although returned to civilian life, the Greenbrier was to maintain a covert connection with the federal government for many years. Beneath its sweeping verandas and graceful rooms, the hotel housed a 112,000-square-foot bunker built in the event that it should ever be necessary to evacuate Congress from the capital. The secret facility, constructed between 1959 and 1962, was declassified in 1995 and is now open for tours.

Today, the Greenbrier continues its spa legacy by operating a comprehensive diagnostic clinic. Guests can come for a full work-up, thoughtfully scheduled around swimming, golf, tennis, horseback riding and of course, cocktails. The Greenbrier's bar, the Old White Lounge, dates to the decommissioning of the property as an army hospital in the 1940s. Initially designed by the celebrated Dorothy Draper, its mid-century chic has been maintained by her successor Carleton Varney, who now runs Dorothy Draper & Co. Paneled in pecky cedar and illuminated by large crystal chandeliers, the room is both smart and simple. In fine weather, the adjacent garden—visible through a string of windows—serves as the scene of alfresco cocktail parties.

THE OLD WHITE LOUNGE (IN 1948, PREVIOUS PAGE AND 1962, OPPOSITE) ALWAYS SPORTED A VERY SNAPPY LOOK THANKS TO THE TALENT OF NOTED INTERIOR DESIGNER, DOROTHY DRAPER.

THE BREAKERS

Juan Ponce de León discovered Florida, but it was Henry Morrison Flagler, a partner in John D. Rockefeller's Standard Oil Company, who really put it on the map. He bought and built railroads and erected hotels from St. Augustine to Miami, making the Sunshine State the getaway destination of choice for moneyed America. Of course, even the leisure class doesn't recreate the way it once did, and Walt Disney World defines downtime in Florida as much or more than the ritzy beach clubs of the past. But in Palm Beach, a town that still knows how to make the rest of the world go away, the Breakers stands as a legacy of Flagler's high-end ambition.

Rising majestically at the terminus of a quarter-mile entry drive, the Breakers first opened its doors on December 29, 1926. Twelve hundred laborers had worked around the clock for twelve months to ready the seven-story hotel for the season. Why the rush? To continue the tradition of hospitality that Flagler established when he first built on this site in 1896. That property, initially known as the Palm Beach Inn and renamed the Breakers in 1901, burned in 1903 and was rebuilt the following year. Fire struck again in 1925, and although Flagler was not around to see his hotel rise again (he died in 1913), rise it did—beautifully.

Designed by the firm Schultz and Weaver, which later designed the second Waldorf-Astoria, the Pierre, and the Sherry Netherland hotels in New York, the Breakers is inspired by the architectural glories of the Italian Renaissance. Its twin-towered façade recalls the Villa Medici in Rome; its grand interior spaces draw from such sources as the Palazzo Carega in Genoa. The mammoth Florentine Dining Room, from which the Tapestry Bar was carved in 1995, is patterned after the fourteenth-century Palazzo Davanzati in Florence.

While outfitted as a very comfortable living room with plush, oversize furniture, the Tapestry Bar is an unmistakably grand space. Eighteen-foot ceilings, impressive chandeliers, a bar constructed from the mantelpiece of a stately English property, and two eighteenth-century French tapestries combine to make cocktail hour here a positively regal affair.

THE BREAKERS
ONE SOUTH COUNTRY ROAD
PALM BEACH, FLORIDA
561.655.6611

CARIBBEAN-SPICED BLACKBERRY COCKTAIL
DRINK RECIPE 19

THE EMERALD MARTINI
DRINK RECIPE 20

FROM ITS ENTRY DRIVE AND LOBBY TO THE BAR AND COURTYARD, THE BREAKERS HAS LONG WOWED GUESTS, SUCH AS
THIS WELL-DRESSED FOURSOME IN THE 1950S.

THE SEELBACH

L ouisville's Seelbach Hotel was the crowning achievement of hotelier siblings Louis and Otto Seelbach. Older brother Louis opened a restaurant in the city at Tenth and Main streets in the early 1870s. By 1880, he'd moved his operation to a larger location, and in 1886, along with brother Otto, got into the hotel business by offering accommodations above the restaurant. It was here, according to a souvenir brochure published in 1900, that the wildly popular Charles Dickens found himself less than welcome. While checking in he was hospitably greeted by the manager. "Having explained his purpose and his relation to his guest," the story goes, the manager was met with this off-putting response, "'When I want you I will send for you.'" With that, Dickens' bags were put on the sidewalk, and the illustrious author was invited to join them.

The Seelbachs' business continued to grow. In 1902, the brothers secured financing for the larger and more elegant hotel that stands today. A Beaux Arts beauty with a grand lobby, Venetian-inspired dining room, and a Spanish Renaissance-style bar featuring a cedar trellis and a ceiling painted with grapevines, the new hotel opened on May 1, 1905, just in time for the running of the Kentucky Derby. Although the bibulous F. Scott Fitzgerald reportedly passed out on the hotel's ballroom floor during one of his visits, the status of this grand hotel did not escape him. In *The Great Gatsby*, Fitzgerald recalls Daisy's social ascent by noting:

In June she married Tom Buchanan of Chicago with more pomp and circumstance than Louisville ever knew before. He came down with a hundred people in four private cars and hired a whole floor of the Seelbach Hotel . . .

In 1907, the brothers installed a many-vaulted rathskeller; its floors, columns, and walls were covered in earthenware created by the renowned Rookwood Pottery of Cincinnati. Put out of business by Prohibition, this popular tavern reopened in 1934, with six bartenders at the ready behind its fifty-six-foot bar. In the 1940s, the space became a Legionnaires' clubroom and later served as an entertainment venue. Today it is reserved for special functions.

The room that now houses the Old Seelbach Bar (upstairs, off the lobby) also has gone through a few changes over the decades. In the 1930s, it was a drugstore. In 1941, it became the Plantation Room, a nightclub that featured a revolving dance floor and a fanciful twenty-five-foot diorama of classical figures and plantation life. "I have had on two different occasions," notes concierge Larry Johnson, "old-timers,

THE SEELBACH
500 FOURTH AVENUE
LOUISVILLE, KENTUCKY
502.585.3200

SEELBACH COCKTAIL
DRINK RECIPE 21

THE BAR OF THE SEELBACH HOTEL HAS SHED ITS SKIN TIME AND AGAIN OVER THE YEARS, BUT AS THESE IMAGES ATTEST, HOSPITALITY WAS NEVER WANTING IN THE BLUEGRASS STATE.

people eighty, eighty-five, who told me when they drank in there it looked like the features of the diorama were moving. But I guess after you drink enough, anything seems like it's moving."

The space was converted to a steakhouse in the 1950s, and later became a bank. It assumed its current incarnation in 1982. In comparison to the Seelbach's soaring lobby, the Old Seelbach Bar seems almost subterranean. A broad space with a low ceiling, the room is decorated with equestrian prints—a reminder that you're in horse country—and is dominated by a hand-

some bar running the width of the room.

Like many small and midsize cities, Louisville has seen much of its life siphoned off to the suburbs over the years, leaving the urban center downright deserted after 6 PM. Although the Old Seelbach Bar can be pretty quiet some nights, the room does get its TGIF crowd, and has begun to enjoy a budding popularity as a late-night spot for jazz on the weekends. The bar carries an impressive array of bourbons—this is Kentucky after all—and has instituted bourbon flights to its program. And you certainly don't need a crowd to enjoy that.

47

THE FAIRMONT NEW ORLEANS

Like the martini and the mint julep, the Sazerac is one of those cocktails whose charms elicit near poetry from its admirers. Poetry and then some. In *The Gentlemen's Companion: Being an Exotic Drinking Book or, Around the World with Jigger, Beaker and Flask*, bon vivant Charles H. Baker, Jr., avers, "It is a sad and shocking fact that more people who should know more know less about this truly remarkable drink than is reasonable—heaven knows why." Before firmly leading his reader through the proper recipe, he pleads, "never try to vary it; for if you do you'll not be drinking a true Sazerac—just some liquid abortion fit only to pour down drains."

You can order a Sazerac just about anywhere in New Orleans, but call for one in the bar of the Fairmont hotel and you place yourself in a direct line to the drink's long history. It was first concocted in the 1830s by a French Quarter apothecary named Antoine Peychaud, whose mixologist instincts led him to combine brandy and absinthe with a dash of the bitters that still bear his name. The drink caught on and in 1853 became known as the Sazerac, when Sewell Taylor, who owned the Sazerac Coffeehouse in Exchange Alley, served it up using Sazerac de Forge et fils brandy. (Some accounts suggest absinthe wasn't included in the drink until the 1870s, when rye whisky also replaced the cognac.)

In 1870, Thomas H. Handy bought the Sazerac Coffeehouse and began marketing various spirits. He acquired the rights to Peychaud's bitters, and in the 1890s, started bottling the Sazerac, as well as running the Sazerac Bar on Royal Street. A successor Sazerac Bar operated at 300 Carondelet Street until 1949 when the Roosevelt Hotel, as the Fairmont was then known, acquired license to the Sazerac name and recipe from what Handy now called the Sazerac Company. The hotel opened its own Sazerac Bar on the Baronne Street side of the hotel in September of that year. In 1958, the bar was moved to its present location in the hotel, replacing an existing barroom were the notorious governor and U.S. Senator Huey Long once held court.

The Fairmont's Sazerac Bar is adorned with murals executed by Louisiana artist Paul Ninas in the 1930s that add to the room's Art Deco ambiance. The four paintings depict life in the Big Easy, as well as celebrities of the era: Edward VIII and that fine Southern lady, Wallis Simpson, Gloria Vanderbilt (in furs), and Groucho Marx. The bar itself measures forty-five feet and is sheathed in African walnut and topped in mahogany.

Think New Orleans and you image wild times, the colorful chaos of Bourbon Street. But as residents and savvy out-of-towners know, there's a place to sip without getting silly—the Sazerac.

THE FAIRMONT NEW ORLEANS
123 BARONNE STREET
NEW ORLEANS, LOUISIANA
504.529.7111

THE SAZERAC COCKTAIL (SIGNATURE DRINK)
DRINK RECIPE 22

THE HOTEL MONTELEONE

"What were they *thinking?*" one is tempted to cry upon encountering the merry-go-round in the Monteleone's Carousel Bar. There's something shocking about seeing this symbol of childhood in a grown-up room. At the same time, it perfectly captures New Orleans' pervasive playfulness, which makes even adults act like kids.

The twenty-four-seat, revolving carousel has been the centerpiece of this barroom, which overlooks Royal Street, since 1949. It's wildly fanciful today, like something straight out of P. T. Barnum, but in the past it sported a simpler, umbrellalike canopy and, at one point, had no canopy at all.

The Hotel Monteleone started life in 1886 when shoe manufacturer Antonio Monteleone bought the sixty-four-room Commercial Hotel at the corner of Royal and Iberville streets in the French Quarter. Several years later, he acquired a second hotel nearby

and in 1908, the combined property took his name. The Monteleone, which has expanded five times over the past 117 years, remains a family-owned business.

The Monteleone has hosted some of the South's greatest writers, including William Faulkner, Tennessee Williams, and Eudora Welty. Truman Capote was almost born on the premises; his mother went into labor during a stay in 1924.

Recalling a visit to the Carousel Bar with his parents, Pulitzer Prize-winning novelist Richard Ford told the *Times-Picayune*, "Suddenly my father got a look of profound consternation on his face. And he said, 'My God, I might have gotten drunk here.' And my mother said, 'Whatever do you mean?' 'I mean that one drink's gone to my head. When I came in this bar, I thought we were on the other side of the room.' He had no idea, sweet man that he was, that the bar was just slowly inching around."

THE HOTEL MONTELEONE
214 ROYAL STREET
NEW ORLEANS, LOUISIANA
504.523.3341

THE VIEUX CARRÉ COCKTAIL (SIGNATURE DRINK)
DRINK RECIPE 23

THE MIDWEST

ILLINOIS **CHICAGO** OMNI AMBASSADOR EAST HOTEL THE DRAKE HOTEL	**53**
OHIO **CINCINNATI** HILTON CINCINNATI NETHERLAND PLAZA HOTEL	**59**
WISCONSIN **MILWAUKEE** THE PFISTER HOTEL	**60**

OMNI AMBASSADOR EAST HOTEL

Most hotel bars serve food. Many are in fact attached to a dining room. But taking a drink in one does not always lead to dinner in the other. Not even at the Pump Room, where the bar and dining room occupy the same space. That's one of the great pleasures of the place; you can stop in for just a drink and still enjoy the show that is the Pump Room's stock-in-trade.

Making an entrance is part of the Pump Room experience. It has been since hotelier Ernie Byfield opened the room in 1938. The bar, which overlooks the dining room, serves as a sort of foyer in the see-and-be-seen promenade that has long been a part of fine dining. After passing through the bar, patrons descend to the formally appointed dining room, which was inspired, Byfield claimed, by the Pump Room in Bath, England, where ladies and gentlemen socialized while sipping the health-enhancing waters. Elevated above the diners, bar patrons are equally on display, so even if you're not here to sup, you are both a player and spectator in the little drama that is the Pump Room.

Byfield and business partner Frank West Bering built the Ambassador East Hotel in the city's affluent Gold Coast district in 1926. The Pump Room was Byfield's effort to create in Chicago the kind of high-profile dining spot more commonly encountered in New York and Los Angeles. Taking advantage of the fact that transcontinental train travel required a stopover in the Windy City, Byfield was able to lure the biggest names of stage and screen to his new room. Renowned tippler John Barrymore was a regular (and his drinks were regularly watered), as were Judy Garland, Humphrey Bogart and Lauren Bacall, Bette Davis, Marilyn Monroe, and Frank Sinatra. These folks and many more—from Robert Frost and Rudolf Nureyev to Susan Sarandon and Kevin Spacey—are celebrated in a panoply of black-and-white photographs in the entrance and throughout the bar.

Byfield was an innkeeper of the old school, as colorful as any of his guests and his idea of swank was as much about showmanship as it was about good taste. He attired his waiters in red swallowtail coats and knee britches, and did up busboys in long jackets and plumed caps as if they were attending Indian rajahs. As for the food, epicure Lucius Beebe wrote, "Almost everything . . . is either stewed in vintage cognac, trimmed with the finest black mushrooms, or bedeviled beyond all reason with garlic, port, and Major Grey's chutney." When it came to presentation, Byfield loved to set dishes aflame, serve them on skewers, or deliver meals to the table on wheels.

Unlike some hotel bars attached to a dining room, the bar at the Pump Room is not a pitiful little

OMNI AMBASSADOR EAST HOTEL
1301 NORTH STATE PARKWAY
CHICAGO, ILLINOIS
312.787.7200

BULL SHOT
DRINK RECIPE 24

waiter's station stuck between the coat check and the kitchen door. No, the taproom here is a good size space with a huge, three-sided bar, tables perfect for tête-a-têtes, and plenty of room to circulate. The clientele here is a loyal one; some neighborhood patrons have been popping in for decades. "One customer we know first came here many years ago as a young woman," relates bartender Angel Romero. "She loved the place and told herself, 'when I get married, I'm going to have my reception here.' Well, last year, she got married and she took the whole room. She even brought back the piano player and singer who appeared here all those years ago. That was some night."

WHILE OVER-THE-TOP UNIFORMS (CIRCA 1943, ABOVE) WERE A PUMP ROOM TRADEMARK FOR DECADES, THE AMBASSADOR EAST LOBBY (RIGHT) HAS ALWAYS BEEN A SOBER SPOT.

RESIDENTS OF CHICAGO'S GOLD COAST FREQUENTLY MAKE THEMSELVES AT HOME IN THE COQ D'OR'S BANQUETTES OR AT THE BAR.

THE DRAKE HOTEL

December 6, 1933. Prohibition ended in Illinois, and the Drake Hotel's Coq d'Or bar was ready to serve a thirsty city. Although repeal was announced at 8:30 PM, people began lining up outside long before that. To handle the rush, Drake bartenders poured whisky—and nothing else—at 40 cents a glass. The hotel had two hundred thousand gallons for the celebration and the party went on all night. The Coq d'Or remains very accommodating, its Midwestern hospitality most evident in The Executive, a four-ounce serving of whatever you're having (twice the size of a standard drink at the Coq d'Or).

The Coq d'Or has changed little over the years. Its design blends allusions to both a ship's cabin—captain's chairs and nautical lanterns—and the solid comfort of an old New England merchant's home—dark wood paneling and pewter mugs and pitchers.

A mural of clipper ships in a harbor recalls the Asian export trade that kept the Yankees of Salem and New Bedford living large. Another mural depicts top-hatted gents and ladies in bonnets gathered on a hillside to watch smartly attired troops assembled in the valley below. All in all, it's a very snug room.

Although situated in a swank hotel, steps from Lake Michigan and adjacent to some of Chicago's finest retailers, the Coq d'Or remains a neighborhood bar. "We have the same people almost every day," observes bartender Kevin Creighton. "Most of them live within just a couple blocks. I know their phone numbers. If they don't show up, sometimes we actually call them. There are times when that's all I have at the bar, regular customers."

Even the Coq d'Or's menu has that place-around-the-corner-hominess; corned beef hash, Bookbinder's soup, and turkey with mashed potatoes and gravy.

THE DRAKE HOTEL
140 EAST WALTON PLACE
CHICAGO, ILLINOIS
312.787.2200

ORANGE OASIS
DRINK RECIPE 25

HILTON CINCINNATI NETHERLAND PLAZA HOTEL

The public spaces of a great hotel are like movie sets. There is nothing ordinary about them and we feel far from ordinary when we inhabit them. Special environments designed to make us feel special, they add a sense of drama to even the simplest activities—taking tea, reading the paper, or ordering a cocktail. This is true no matter what the hotel's décor. But if there's one aesthetic that really makes you feel like a star, it's Art Deco and for that, the Hilton Cincinnati Netherland Plaza can't be beat.

The Netherland Plaza is a component of Carew Tower, a mixed-use development that opened in 1931. The work of architect Walter W. Ahlschlager and his chief designer, George Unger, the hotel is a showplace embellished with German silver (a copper, zinc, and nickel alloy), Brazilian rosewood, and Rookwood pottery. When Winston Churchill stayed at the hotel in 1933, he waxed poetic over the city. "From the tower of its unsurpassed hotel, the city spreads far and wide its pageant of crimson, purple, and gold laced by silver streams that are great rivers." What's more, it's said the great statesman was so struck by the green tile and silver leaf décor of his bathroom at the hotel that he had it replicated in his country home.

The Palm Court Bar, which has occupied a section of the lobby since 1983, is a visually and spatially impressive manifestation of the Art Deco spirit. It is assertive, energetic, and makes anyone sitting in it feel more attractive and sophisticated. The gold leaf, rich reflective wood, elaborate sconces, and a ceiling that soars more than twenty feet so fully capture the stylish formality of the past, you almost wonder why every gentleman present isn't in a suit and every woman wearing a hat.

HILTON CINCINNATI NETHERLAND PLAZA HOTEL
35 WEST FIFTH STREET
CINCINNATI, OHIO
513.421.9100

STINGER
DRINK RECIPE 26

CAFÉ NETHERLAND
DRINK RECIPE 27

THE PFISTER HOTEL

Ah, Milwaukee—land of beer and bratwurst! Well, brats remain a staple (and a damn good one, at that) but most of the breweries have long since departed. Like other older cities that have seen their primary industries fade and their populations shift to the suburbs, Milwaukee is reinventing itself. Nineteenth- and early twentieth-century factories and warehouses are being retrofitted as high-end housing and the locals have learned anew that eating out and shopping well are a good part of what city living is all about. This sense of the city as a place to revel in, rather than run from, is certainly something earlier Milwaukeeans appreciated. After all, Milwaukee was thriving long before Chicago big-shouldered its way to national prominence. Its successful tanners, brewers, and grain merchants lived in fine mansions, and beginning in 1893, exhibited themselves socially at the Pfister Hotel.

Erected by immigrant Guido Pfister, who made a fortune in tanning before getting into the hospitality business, the Pfister is a solid Romanesque Revival edifice with a vaulted, triple-story lobby. When it opened, the hotel boasted a formal dining room dominated by an impressive bar, and a gentlemen's lounge with its own bar (there were also two billiard rooms, one for each sex). In 1926, Pfister's son Charles opened the English Room, a small pub serving steaks and chops; he even invented a house specialty he called Indian Punch, which he had hoped to bottle and sell nationwide.

In the 1950s, a good piece of the lobby was closed off and turned into a lounge called The Columns, where toga-clad waitresses served drinks and a centurion watched the door. Later renamed Café Olé, it remained in place until the 1990s, when preparations were made to restore the hotel for its centennial in 1993. Olé's walls came down and the lobby reassumed the graceful grandeur it had possessed 100 years earlier.

Although there was no bar in the lobby when the hotel first opened, the owners have successfully created one without compromising the Victorian-era opulence that makes the Pfister one of the grand hotels of the Midwest. Set off by a low, wrought-iron railing patterned after those that ornament the grand staircase and mezzanine, the Lobby Lounge is anchored at one end by a large hearth hood studded with ornamental grapes and cherubs. The entrance is marked by the figures of two insouciant pikemen cast in bronze.

The space is outfitted with plump sofas and black lacquer chairs and is punctuated by faux marble columns topped with gilded capitals that join with the golden-hued walls to create a pervasive, jewellike glow. Sitting in the Lobby Lounge, one feels awash in that exquisite luminosity that descends at the end of a perfect summer's day.

THE PFISTER HOTEL
424 EAST WISCONSIN AVENUE
MILWAUKEE, WISCONSIN
414.273.8222

APPLE MARTINI
DRINK RECIPE 28

FRENCH 75
DRINK RECIPE 29

THE ARIZONA BILTMORE

The Arizona Biltmore was a family affair. Midwestern brothers Charles and Warren MacArthur arrived in Arizona in 1910 and 1913, respectively, and within a few years had formed the Arizona Hotel Company. But their ambition to build a resort outside Phoenix was thwarted by the impending war, and it wasn't until the late '20s that they were able raise the necessary capital. In 1929, thanks in part to the investment of the Chicago chewing-gum magnate William Wrigley, Jr.—who later became the project's majority stockholder—the Arizona Biltmore opened its doors. Designed by the developers' eldest sibling, architect Albert Chase MacArthur, the hotel is perhaps the most famous building Frank Lloyd Wright did not build.

The confusion was cast from the start. Albert Chase MacArthur, trained at Harvard and the Armour Institute (now the Illinois Institute of Technology), had apprenticed to Mr. Wright. When he was devising his scheme for the Biltmore, he decided to use ornamental concrete blocks inspired by those Wright had used on the Millard House in Pasadena, and at Wright's urging, engaged the senior architect as a consultant. As a result, the Biltmore, Albert Chase MacArthur's only major building, has often been perceived as one of Wright's own. To his great credit, Wright ultimately wrote a letter disavowing authorship.

Wright's five months on-site were a trying period for both men. Wright's wife, Olgivianna, later recalled, "It was a very difficult task for him since my husband,

as we all know, was never famous as a man who willingly made any compromises." MacArthur himself admitted that when the building was finished, Wright dismissed it as even worse than he thought it would be. Despite the slam, when *Architectural Record* ran a story on the hotel, MacArthur sent a copy of the magazine to Wright with the note, "To F. L.W., my master, without whose aid the Biltmore would hardly have been possible."

Nonetheless, the notion that the Biltmore was Wright's handiwork persisted. It didn't help matters when Taliesin West, the studio Wright had established near Phoenix in 1938, was hired to work on the property following a fire in 1973. And over time, some distinctly Wrightian touches—carpeting he had designed for his Imperial Hotel in Tokyo, stained glass murals, and various characteristic furnishings—came to adorn the Biltmore.

Built as an accommodating retreat for the affluent, the Biltmore exploited a Wild West motif in its early years. At its debut, James Woods, vice president of the Arizona Biltmore Corporation, circled in a plane overhead and dropped a bouquet of roses con-

THE ARIZONA BILTMORE RESORT & SPA
2400 EAST MISSOURI
PHOENIX, ARIZONA
602.955.6600

THE BILTMORE COSMOPOLITAN (SIGNATURE DRINK)
DRINK RECIPE 30

taining a gold key to the throng below. His aim was awry and the precious bundle landed on the hotel roof, where a Filipino employee, tricked out like a Hopi Indian for the gala, retrieved it. Though no dude ranch, the hotel's logo sported a bucking bronco and its doorman wore a ten-gallon hat.

Although born during Prohibition, the Biltmore didn't entirely neglect its thirsty guests. For patrons who brought their own hooch, the hotel provided a 'set-up'—glasses, ice, and mixers. And as at most hotels during the dry spell, someone somewhere on the premises knew how to deliver the goods to those who failed to pack their own.

The Biltmore, now called a resort and spa, has housed several bars over the decades, including the Aztec Room with a jewellike ceiling in gold leaf. Today, guests gather in the Squaw Peak Lounge, named for the mountain that rises above the property. While outfitted in the walnut-paneled mode of a club-room, the lounge is graced by generous windows and leads to an adjacent patio, offering an embrace of the outdoors that is key to the Biltmore experience.

A RUGGED GRACE CHARMED THE BILTMORE'S GUESTS IN THE EARLY YEARS (LEFT). THE MIX OF EARTHY MATERIALS AND BOLD FABRICS AT PLAY IN THE SQUAW PEAK LOUNGE CONTINUE THAT BOLD DECORATIVE TRADITION (RIGHT).

THE HOTEL JEROME

W hen the first silver prospectors trudged into Ute territory in 1879, hitting the hay at the end of the day meant crawling into a tent. A decade later, that rugged camp called Aspen had become a city and successful miners were bedding down in the Hotel Jerome.

The dream of two innkeepers from Kansas, the Hotel Jerome got started when New Yorker Jerome B. Wheeler kicked in $60,000 and a parcel of land for the project. Wheeler, a noted Civil War veteran and the president of R. H. Macy & Co., had ventured West in hopes that the mountain air would restore his wife's health. But he didn't spend his time playing nursemaid. He invested in local mines, established Aspen's first bank, and financed the area's first hydroelectric plant. When the hotel's construction costs skyrocketed and Wheeler's partners skipped town, he saw the job through to the end.

With its steam heat, electric lights, and artfully appointed public spaces, the Jerome was the pride of Aspen when it opened in November 1889. But its promise, like the city's itself, was short-lived. The repeal of the Sherman Silver Act and the return of the gold standard in 1893 hurt the whole town. Wheeler declared bankruptcy in 1903; he lost the Jerome to back taxes six years later. Aspen's population dropped from 12,000 in 1893 to 700 in 1935. Although the silver-mining days were over, there were always a few folks who clung unscrupulously to the past. One wily entrepreneur continued to sell worthless mining stock

at ten cents a share. When business was good, he'd buy drinks all around at the Jerome.

The Jerome struggled to stay open through the first decade of the new century. With fewer guests, the bar was one of the only spots in the hotel to see any business, thanks to Mansor Elisha, a former traveling salesman who took over the operation of the hotel in 1910 and bought it a year later. But it would be thirty-five years before things really started to look up. In 1946, Chicagoan Walter Paepcke, president of the Container Corporation of America, leased the property with an eye to making Aspen a retreat for intellectuals and business leaders. He brought in the Bauhaus-trained Herbert Bayer to renovate the hotel, and before long, bright minds (Albert Schweitzer, Mortimer Adler) and big stars (Lana Turner, John Wayne) were checking in. In the fifties, the Aspen Institute, the Aspen Music Festival and School, and the International Design Conference were all founded at the Jerome.

Whether visiting movers and shakers wanted to kick around a few ideas or just kick back, the hotel's J-Bar was one comfortable place to do it. Still is. Step in and you'll see Gucci-clad swells sipping next to construction workers (and maybe journalist Hunter S.

THE HOTEL JEROME
330 EAST MAIN STREET
ASPEN, COLORADO
970.920.1000

ASPEN CRUD (SIGNATURE DRINK)
DRINK RECIPE 31

Thompson enjoying a *hefty* Chivas on the rocks).

During Prohibition, the barroom was converted to a soda fountain. After Repeal, it apparently functioned as both bar and soda fountain. When the Army's 10th Mountain Division bunked at the hotel during World War II, resourceful soldiers took advantage of both services to create what has become the J-Bar's signature drink, the Aspen Crud—an innocent-looking milkshake laced with bourbon.

In 2000, the J-Bar was rejuvenated to recall the room in its early days. The 111-year-old bar itself was carefully restored. Crafted by Chinese artisans, with delicate tracery and pagodalike shapes, the bar's design comes as a surprise in this otherwise very Victorian hotel. For more than a century, bartenders have taken to inscribing their names in one of its drawers. One now-anonymous fellow started it all when he carved, "I opened Jerome bar, 1889."

THE BROWN PALACE HOTEL

It's disheartening to enter a fine old hotel and discover that its bar has been decoratively dumbed down; strung with Route 66 memorabilia, festooned with beer signage and outfitted for the sports fan, or done up to resemble the set of *Cheers* or someone's idea of a Third Avenue saloon (right down to the spittoon). Themed to the max, these bars have little to do with the hotel's true character. But, in fact, many of the old hotel bars were theme rooms to begin with. After all, American hotel architecture was essentially an imitative art, executed in the Beaux Arts tradition, which was itself aping the past. These public spaces were meant to conjure the princely splendor of a château, or the hushed significance of a gentlemen's club. Decades before the Best Westerning of America, however, some hoteliers opted for bars that did not evoke a Belle Epoque salon or the sanctum of a Gilded Age industrialist—even when the hotels they ran were built in those eras.

If the Ship Tavern occupied the premises of a sea-side resort or the Parker House in Boston, its celebration of the clipper ship would be spot on. But situated within a stupendous Italian Renaissance edifice in land-locked Denver (a city shaped by the Colorado gold rush of 1859), it comes as something of a surprise.

Henry Cordes Brown, an Ohio carpenter who came west and made his fortune in real estate, opened the Brown Palace in 1892. Designed by Frank E. Edbrooke, who also did Denver's State Capitol, the Brown surrounds a dramatic atrium eight stories tall and enclosed by wrought-iron railings. The Ship Tavern itself did not appear until 1934, when it took over a space once occupied by the ladies' tearoom. The Brown's owner at the time, sugar and cement

THE BROWN PALACE HOTEL
321 SEVENTEENTH STREET
DENVER, COLORADO
303.297.3111

TAVERN COFFEE
DRINK RECIPE 32

magnate C. K. Boettcher, collected maritime material and after Repeal, he decided to put in a bar and dining room decorated with some of his treasures. (Besides, Mrs. Boettcher wasn't keen on keeping his haul at home.)

Although the bar—with its ship models, Jamaican rum barrels, and a complete mast and crow's nest—does nothing to conjure the rugged West, it has seen its share of frontier behavior, reminders of the days when outlaws and desperadoes walked Denver's streets. In the autumn of 1946, a World War II veteran went wild with a pistol, killing one patron and wounding two others. And when the National Western Stock Show and Rodeo arrives in town, commotion comes a-callin'. "We used to get the rodeo cowboys in here," recalls long-time waiter Tom Baines. "Now the cattlemen are all right, but when the rodeo cowboys come in, there's always a fight."

THE BROWN PALACE DOMINATED DOWNTOWN DENVER IN ITS EARLY YEARS (LEFT). TODAY, THE JAUNTY SHIP TAVERN LOOKS MUCH AS IT DID WHEN IT OPENED IN 1934.

THE OXFORD HOTEL

Despite war and the Depression, the 1930s still occupy the popular imagination as the most glamorous age in American culture, especially when it comes to cocktails and good times. Everyone seems to have a sense of what those increasingly distant days were all about, thanks to innumerable films photographed on streamlined sets and New York City streets. Although the physical chic of the period—slinky gowns, dinner jackets, and Art Deco interiors—is often associated with Manhattan or Los Angeles, the look swept across the country. Even Denver, which in mid-century seemed mighty far from the cosmopolitan doings of the coasts, boasted the very stylish Cruise Room in the Oxford Hotel.

Like the Menger Hotel in Austin, Texas, the Oxford was the project of a brewer, Denver's Adolph Zang. The work of Colorado architect Frank E. Edbrooke, who designed Denver's Brown Palace Hotel a year later, the Oxford opened its doors in 1891. Its amenities included up-to-date water closets and a saloon pouring Zang's own Fritz Imperial beer.

Expanded in 1902 and again in 1912, the hotel went Deco in the 1930s when Denver architect Charles Jaka remodeled it. Among Jaka's contributions was the Cruise Room cocktail lounge. In today's parlance, "cruise" suggests a certain sexual outing, but the room, and its name, were in fact inspired by the lounges of the Queen Mary which is now docked in Long Beach, California.

Jaka outfitted the space with chrome, lacquer, and the neon lighting that gives the room its flattering pink glow. With just eight booths and eight stools at the bar, the Cruise Room is a very intimate space.

By the 1960s lower downtown Denver had gone bust and the Oxford was renting rooms at fifty cents a night. In 1979, preservationist developer Charles Callaway purchased the hotel. The following year, fellow preservationist Dana Crawford invested in the property, and together the two saw to it that the Oxford and its Cruise Room were made shipshape. In the past fifteen years, the entire distict—now known as LoDo—has emerged as a trendy area of restaurants, retailers, and galleries. The Cruise Room has long attracted a mature patron who enjoys an Old Fashioned or Whiskey Sour. Now on the weekends, the bar is wall-to-wall with a younger crowd that comes as much for new-fangled martinis as it does for the ambiance.

THE OXFORD HOTEL
1600 17TH STREET
DENVER, COLORADO
303.628.5400

BACARDI COCKTAIL
DRINK RECIPE 33

NEGRONI
DRINK RECIPE 34

ROB ROY
DRINK RECIPE 35

THE RICHLY ORNAMENTED FAÇADE OF THE DRISKILL HOTEL IS AN INSPIRING SIGHT IN DOWNTOWN AUSTIN (LEFT). TRADITIONAL AND CONTEMPORARY FURNISHINGS, CACTI, AND WESTERN-THEMED ACCESSORIES GIVE THE DRISKILL'S BAR AN UNMISTAKABLE TEXAN ACCENT (RIGHT).

THE DRISKILL HOTEL

The history of the Driskill Hotel reads like Elizabeth Taylor's medical records. The property changed hands at least a dozen times since its debut in 1886, closed down more than once, and faced demolition in 1969. As for its bar, well, between Prohibition and the state's laws that restricted the selling of liquor by the glass to supper clubs, it went without one for years. Today, the bar comes off like a cleaned-up version of what an old-time saloon was all about, but folks don't come here to ooh and ahh over authentic décor.

The hotel was built by Tennessee-born cattleman Jesse Lincoln Driskill, who made his first big money selling stock to the Confederacy. The Driskill opened in December and closed in May, when manager S. E. McIlhenny, wooed to work for Galveston's Beach Hotel, took off with half the staff, including bartender Joe Cooley, "the jolly genius of the Driskill bar." Nonetheless, within those few months, the hotel had proved attractive to both Governor Sul Ross, who held his inaugural ball at the hotel (as would many of his successors), and pool shark L. L. Magnus, who hustled in the Driskill's billiard parlor.

Over the years, the hotel witnessed the schemes of itinerant snake oilers R. C. and A. H. Flowers of Boston (the duo offered diagnoses via their "intuitive gifts"), the efforts of the Daughters of the Republic of Texas to save the Alamo as a historic site, and the strategizing of the Texas Rangers who executed the fatal ambush of outlaws Bonnie and Clyde. In 1934, Lyndon Baines Johnson courted Lady Bird over breakfast at the Driskill. LBJ was back again and again, awaiting election returns for his senate run in 1948, his vice presidential bid in 1960, and his own presidential run in 1964. More recently, during George W. Bush's campaign for the White House, the Driskill bar was awash with media and politicos, from newsman Bernard Shaw to soon-to-be Vice President Dick Cheney.

A long, saloonlike space with a pressed copper ceiling, a seven-sided bar, a carpet "branded" with the letter D, and light fixtures fashioned from old pistols and spurs, the Driskill bar doesn't buzz with that kind of energy every day, but it is unquestionably, Austin's premier hotel bar.

THE DRISKILL HOTEL
604 BRAZOS STREET
AUSTIN, TEXAS
512.474.5911

7TH STREET COSMO BLANCO (SIGNATURE DRINK)
DRINK RECIPE 36

THE HOTEL ADOLPHUS AND
THE MELROSE HOTEL

There are bars in Texas where one can ride a mechanical bull and occasionally hear some well-lubricated local yell "Yee-haw!" And while such places may be more for the tenderfoot than the real McCoy, the state still strikes the outsider as a wide open expanse, rough and new. George W. Bush takes a certain pride in that image, extolling the virtues of life in the dusty little town of Crawford. But many Texans take greater pride in the oil-infused luxe of Dallas, where a well-rigged propriety rivals that of many Eastern cities. Although two of the town's most popular hotel bars are a mere twenty years old, they sit in venerable properties that have been around for much longer. Both are traditional spaces. But one revels in its reputation as a fashionable meeting spot, the other takes satisfaction in its lower key renown as a companion to a highly-rated restaurant.

The bar at the seventy-nine-year-old Melrose Hotel is called the Library. On any given afternoon, one will find Dallasites settled comfortably in its wing chairs, looking very much at home as a pianist softly coaxes the day along. Come evening, hotel guests wander in. The room is so popular that on weekends, a little velvet rope closes off one of its entrances and the wait for a table can last forty-five minutes.

The Hotel Adolphus, built in 1912 by beer baron Adolphus Busch, has housed several supper clubs and taprooms in its ornate premises over the years. Since 1982, its sole saloon has been the elegant French Room Bar, a companion to the hotel's fine dining room. Paneled in walnut, furnished with antiques and oil paintings, and outfitted with a fireplace, the bar (it seems a shame to call it a bar) possesses the well-heeled style of a sumptuously comfortable salon. Mercifully, and unlike so many of the country's better hotel bars, the French Room Bar has yet to install a television.

THE HOTEL ADOLPHUS
1321 COMMERCE STREET
DALLAS, TEXAS
214.742.8200

ADOLPHUS SIDECAR (SIGNATURE DRINK)
DRINK RECIPE 37

THE MELROSE HOTEL
3015 OAK LAWN AVENUE
DALLAS, TEXAS
214.521.5151

THE LIBRARY MARTINI (SIGNATURE DRINK)
DRINK RECIPE 38

THE FRENCH ROOM BAR OF THE HOTEL ADOLPHUS (LEFT) CATERS TO THE DALLAS ESTABLISHMENT WHILE THE LIBRARY
LOUNGE AT THE MELROSE DRAWS A SOPHISTICATED, SEE-AND-BE-SEEN CROWD.

THE MENGER HOTEL

People pop into the bar of the Menger Hotel for any number of reasons. To get out of the heat, sip a margarita, seek directions to the Alamo (this, despite the fact that the historic mission is just steps away), or to ask about the ghost (more on that later). But for history lovers, it's the look of the room that draws them—and the fact that Teddy Roosevelt and his Rough Riders gathered at the Menger before charging up San Juan Hill.

German immigrant William Menger arrived in San Antonio in the 1840s and went into the brewery business. He put up his hotel in 1859 and installed a bar in 1863. With the arrival of the railroad in 1887, the Menger became one of the best known hotels in the Southwest. Although guests enjoyed supping on wild game and snapper soup from turtles caught in the San Antonio River, they found the taproom wanting, so Menger's successor, Herman Kampmann, set out to upgrade the space. And he didn't go for just any old décor with a spittoon on the floor. Instead, he patterned the place after the drinking room in the House of Lords in London, complete with mahogany bar, cherry ceiling, and beveled mirrors from France.

Theodore Roosevelt first visited the Menger while on a hunting trip in 1892. He returned in 1898 as second in command of the 1st U.S. Volunteer Cavalry Regiment, a colorful collection of cowboys, miners, and East Coast swells mustered for duty in the Spanish-American War. The regiment trained in San Antonio and a number of them signed up at a station in the Menger Hotel.

Since TR's day, the Menger bar has peregrinated about the property before coming to rest in its current location in 1949. During Prohibition, bartender George La Motte had its components put in storage and the space was converted to a dress shop. Once the Noble Experiment was over, the bar was back and La Motte with it. A local paper noted at the time, "Like all good bartenders, his first name is George. He parts his hair in the middle and he has a certain look in his eye that makes you think he is the sort of man you want to tell your troubles to along about the fifth drink."

As for ghosts, well, the hotel claims to have at least thirty-two running about the place, including Sallie, a chambermaid who was shot by her husband in 1876. While most seem to linger in the lobby, corridors, and at least one guest room, the bar isn't free of their funny business. The lights flicker and glassware shifts about. "You always try to find a logical explanation for these things," says bar manager Denise Baez. "The building is old, the glasses were wet on the bottom so that's why they slid, but there's one thing I can't explain. It was a night I was closing. All the doors

THE MENGER HOTEL
204 ALAMO PLAZA
SAN ANTONIO, TEXAS
210.223.4361

THE MENGER MARGARITA (SIGNATURE DRINK)
DRINK RECIPE 39

THE MENGER HOTEL'S GLORIOUS LOBBY (LEFT) IS IN MARKED CONTRAST TO THE CLOSE AND PUBLIKE ATMOSPHERE OF ITS BAR, SHOWN HERE IN A PHOTO TAKEN IN THE 1930S.

were locked, I was alone. We have a little balcony in the bar with extra seating. I went up to wipe off the tables there, then came down and was wiping the tables underneath the balcony when I heard the floor above creak. It takes a lot of body weight to make that floor creak. And this was no little patter."

Baez flew out of the bar and didn't return until she had a security person in tow. Although she still gets chills recalling that night, she remains wonderfully good-humored about it and all the odd goings-on at the Menger. "People come in here and ask, 'Where's the ghost?' I say, 'Keep on drinking. You may see two.'"

LA VALENCIA HOTEL

La Jolla was a sleepy little burg when La Valencia opened it doors in 1926. But with its proximity to Los Angeles, magnificent ocean view, and top-drawer service, the hotel quickly drew Hollywood's elite—from Garbo and Gilbert to Lillian Gish and Groucho Marx—all seeking a convenient hideaway. Affectionately known as the "Pink Lady of La Jolla," the Mediterranean-style hotel was erected by local businessmen MacArthur Gorton and Roy B. Wiltsie as La Valencia Apartment-Hotel. Two years later, they dropped the "apartment" and added the tower that so dramatically sets off the building against the sea and sky. (During World War II, Civil Defense personnel manned the tower around the clock, watching the skies for enemy aircraft.)

The hotel's reputation as a celebrity haunt grew in 1947 when La Jolla native Gregory Peck and fellow stars Dorothy McGuire and Mel Ferrer founded the La Jolla Playhouse. Although productions were mounted on the stage of the local high school, that didn't stop an array of big names from making the trip to appear there (and work for the union minimum of $55 a week).

In the mid 1950s, La Valencia opened the Whaling Bar, and this New Bedford–inspired room became the spot for opening night parties. Eartha Kitt, Anne Baxter, Victor Mature, John Wayne, and Jack Lemmon are just a few of the first-night revelers veteran bartender Rey Arcibal served over the years. "I've been with this hotel forty-two years," he notes, "and I never met an actress or an actor who was high falutin'." Of course, when pushed, even a lady like Joan Crawford wouldn't countenance disrespect. When she caught two Whaling Bar patrons commenting on her derriére, she hiked up her skirt to give the catty couple a better look.

Arcibal was taken aback himself when he spotted a man wearing a hat in the bar (this was in the days when men wore hats and knew when to remove them). "He was sitting in one of the booths with a beautiful blonde and I said to the maitre d', 'That man is ridiculous. He doesn't have any etiquette at all.' So the maitre d' says, 'You know who that is?' I said, 'No, I don't know who he is.' 'That's Walter Winchell.'" Winchell never did remove his hat, but then again, he rarely did.

While celebrities always add a certain dash to a room, the best hotel bars are those where local residents feel welcome. The bar at La Valencia has always been a home away from home for La Jollans. Over the years, Arcibal picked up the phone many times to hear, "This is Mrs. So-and-so. Is my husband there?"

Not surprisingly, the Whaling Bar is thematically decorated with harpoons, lanterns, and model ships. The barrel-shaped clock behind the bar was a gift from

LA VALENCIA HOTEL
1132 PROSPECT ST.
LA JOLLA, CALIFORNIA
858.454.0771

THE WHALER (SIGNATURE DRINK)
DRINK RECIPE 40

General Billy Mitchell, the World War I Signal Corps aviator who believed fully in the superiority of air power and fought heatedly with superiors who didn't. Set above the bar is a mural titled *Whale's Last Stand* that depicts a whale hunt off the coast of New England. One of several works local artist Wing Howard executed for the hotel, the picture was cov-

ered over in the 1970s when precursors of today's politically correct crowd expressed dissatisfaction with the all-too-accurate image. *Whale's Last Stand* gave way to a happier scene of a whale escaping its hopeful captors. In 1999, a team from the Getty Museum restored the original and no one it seems, has suffered much since.

BARTENDER REY ARCIBAL, SHOWN HERE IN AN OLD PHOTOGRAPH, CONTINUES TO KEEP CUSTOMERS OF THE WHALING BAR SATISFIED. A BIT OF NEW ENGLAND IN SOUTHERN CALIFORNIA, THE ROOM IS ONE OF THE MOST INVITING SPOTS IN LA JOLLA.

THE HOTEL BEL-AIR

In 1922, developer Alphonso E. Bell snapped up six hundred acres west of Los Angeles and began creating a swank neighborhood he soon christened Bel Air. Bell's creation was a success, so much so that it eventually outclassed nearby Beverly Hills. And the epicenter of this oh-so-exclusive district is the Hotel Bel-Air.

Situated on twelve lush acres, the hotel was originally the sales office for Bell's Bel-Air Estates. In 1946, Texan hotelier Joseph Drown transformed the property into the perfect hideaway for Hollywood's elite and VIPs from around the world. Warren Beatty and the Princess of Wales are just two of the zoom-lens-eluding individuals who sought seclusion here, safely screened behind palm fronds and ficus leaves and a little swan-bedecked lake.

The softly lit bar—a gathering place for local residents, hotel guests, and the film crowd that so often conducts business here—is a clubby room, with mahogany paneling, dark green carpeting, leather upholstery, and a fireplace. Although it's been spruced up—most recently in 1999—it retains the look and feel it possessed when Mr. Drown installed it in the 1940s. Like a good facelift, the renovation left the bar looking just like itself—only better.

Senior bartender Steve Conlin has worked the room for eighteen years and has seen a lot of Hollywood glamour. A pleasantly direct and highly discreet gentleman, he is unfazed at this point by stars and the egotism endemic to the movie industry. "I've been around celebrities my whole working life and, after awhile, the person you don't know is just as interesting as the person who just walked in with an Oscar in his hand." Nonetheless, during his years at the Hotel Bel-Air, even he has been struck by the stars from time to time.

"It was Academy Awards night," he begins, the words setting the stage as effectively in this environment as 'once upon a time' does in the nursery. "The studio had put up this group of people, all of them nominated for a single film—the director, the writer, the actors. It was a politically charged film and they had done very well at other award ceremonies prior to that. This entire group of sixteen people left for the awards ceremony, and since we don't have a television in the bar, I didn't follow how the awards went. Ordinarily, if you're a winner, we don't see you again that evening because there are parties to attend. So, about eleven o'clock, each one of these sixteen people came back to the bar. And all of them wept, because they had all lost. I looked out at this elegant room and at all these elegantly attired people, and the depth of their shock and grief at their loss was something I'd never have imagined. I remember thinking, 'You won't ever see this in the papers.'"

THE HOTEL BEL-AIR
701 STONE CANYON ROAD
LOS ANGELES, CALIFORNIA
310.472.1211

THE BEL-AIR BELLINI (SIGNATURE DRINK)
DRINK RECIPE 41

THE BEVERLY HILLS HOTEL

"**H**alfway between Los Angeles and the sea." That was how developer Burton Green poetically described the address of The Beverly Hills Hotel in the invitations to its grand opening in May 1912. Beverly Hills wasn't yet a city and the "Pink Palace," as the mission-style hotel is fondly known, wasn't even pink; that distinctive cosmetic touch was applied in 1948.

Still surrounded by bean fields in 1914, the triple-towered property accrued its first sheen of glamour in the 1920s when Mary Pickford and Douglas Fairbanks built their famous Pickfair estate on land above the hotel. Soon Gloria Swanson, Charlie Chaplin, Ronald Coleman, Buster Keaton, and many other celluloid luminaries made their way to the still-sleepy town. Humorist Will Rogers was inaugurated Mayor of Beverly Hills on the hotel grounds in 1923. In 1941, Hernando Courtwright (who by then shared ownership of the hotel with Harry Warner and film stars Loretta Young and Irene Dunne) renamed the El Jardin restaurant The Polo Lounge in honor of polo-playing regulars Rogers, Darryl Zanuck, Spencer Tracy, and Tommy Hitchcock.

By now, the hotel's cachet was firmly established. While Howard Hughes hid out in one of the hotel's garden bungalows (ordering pineapple upside down cake at 3 AM), Humphrey Bogart hit the bar. So did Marlene Dietrich, who, true to her gender-bending persona, demolished the no-slacks-for-ladies rule when she showed up for a sip in trousers. In 1949, architect Paul Revere Williams designed a new addition to the hotel and instituted the pink-and-green color scheme that pervades the building to this day.

Come the 1950s, Frank Sinatra, Dean Martin, and other Rat Packers were keeping The Polo Lounge bartenders busier than ever. Today, the lounge continues to draw entertainment industry figures as well as those curious to catch a glimpse of the stars at play. Robert De Niro and Jack Nicholson are among those who command a seat in the see-and-be-seen real estate: booths numbers 1, 2, and 3. "And we have a lot of writers, a lot of music people," notes maitre d' Pepe De Anda. "They like to have their meetings here. I think the new generation tries to follow the same standards, they like the glamour of saying, 'I'll be in The Polo Lounge signing my contract'."

THE BEVERLY HILLS HOTEL
ON SUNSET BOULEVARD
BEVERLY HILLS, CALIFORNIA
310.276.2251

THE PINK PALACE (SIGNATURE DRINK)
DRINK RECIPE 42

THE "PINK PALACE" STANDS TALL AND PROUD AT NINETY-ONE. EQUAL PARTS GLAMOUR AND DISCRETION COMBINE TO MAKE THE POLO LOUNGE AN EVER-POPULAR RETREAT FOR HOLLYWOOD'S ELITE (RIGHT).

MILLENNIUM BILTMORE HOTEL

In Los Angeles, things are not always quite what they appear. This applies to buildings as well as faces. Yet, while film stars take a nip here and a tuck there to appear forever young, the eighty-year-old Millennium Biltmore Hotel has done its best to look its age, even if that means engaging in a little make-believe. The hotel's Gallery Bar, a high-ceilinged room of baronial proportions, looks as if it has held a snuggling Carole Lombard and Clark Gable in its warm wooded embrace. But the bar is a fairly recent creation, developed in the mid-1980s from what had been a grand but very utilitarian corridor.

The Biltmore was the birthplace of the Academy of Motion Picture Arts and Sciences, an idea hatched at an entertainment industry banquet held in the hotel's Crystal Ballroom in 1927 (the Oscar statuette was sketched on a hotel napkin). The Academy's annual awards ceremony was held at the hotel in 1931, and again from 1935 to 1939.

While the Gallery Bar celebrates its motion picture connections with vintage photographs hung on its walls, the room is not really a celebrity hangout but a respite for hotel guests and everyday Angelenos who work downtown. It's the kind of place one might see in countless 1940s movies set in Southern California—*The Best Years of Our Lives*, maybe—films whose characters had nothing to do with Hollywood but who went about their business and enjoyed a cocktail at the end of the day in rooms whose glamour could make anyone feel like a star.

MILLENNIUM BILTMORE HOTEL
506 SOUTH GRAND AVENUE
LOS ANGELES, CALIFORNIA
213.624.1011

BLACK DAHLIA
DRINK RECIPE 43

HOTEL DEL CORONADO

Thanks to its many appearances on film and television—most famously in William Wilder's classic comedy, *Some Like It Hot*, starring Marilyn Monroe—the Hotel Del Coronado is arguably the most recognizable hotel in the country. Gazing at its dormers and turrets and towers, taking dinner in the soaring Crown Room, or riding one of the old Otis elevators, it's possible to imagine The Del's early days when gentlemen guests hunted quail and rabbit nearby and a constitutional after dinner was often the only exercise a lady ever took.

A sprawling pile of red-roofed whiteness, The Del was a project of Midwestern businessmen Elisha Babcock and Hampton Story. In 1885, they purchased the entire peninsula of Coronado—the 5.3-square-mile strip that forms the western boundary of San Diego Bay—for $110,000. After auctioning off lots there in 1886 (they recouped their investment in one day), the two set out to create their resort. Fifteen months and $1 million later, the Hotel Del Coronado welcomed its first guests.

The Del was erected in a time when people came for "the season," staying for weeks and even months each winter, often with nannies and personal maids in tow. The hotel's setting and service and the balmy climate proved positively Edenic, especially to those escaping cold winters back East. Rhapsodizing over a 1905 visit, Henry James wrote, "I live on oranges and olives, fresh from the tree, and I lie awake nights to listen, on purpose, to the languid lisp of the Pacific."

Although battered over the years by economic downturns, war, and changing lifestyles, The Del survived to enjoy a newfound appreciation in the preservationist spirit generated by the nation's bicentennial in 1976. A property that had begun to seem a bit old-fashioned was now revered for its history and charm. In 1998, Lowe Enterprises and Destination Resorts and Hotels, its hotel management subsidiary, began a $55 million restoration of the hotel and its grounds.

Today, the Hotel Del offers guests all the usual amenities, but as with any great hotel, the building itself is the prime amenity. From the eye-beguiling whimsy of its exterior and the lushness of its interior courtyard to the voluminous formality of the dining room, The Del's public spaces are its most appealing assets. Not the least among these is the bar.

When it opened, the *San Diego Tribune* described the bar as "undoubtedly the largest and most elegantly appointed saloon on the coast." A big room facing the ocean, its centerpiece was—and

HOTEL DEL CORONADO
1500 ORANGE AVENUE
CORONADO, CALIFORNIA
619.435.6611

KLONDIKE BAR
DRINK RECIPE 44

SINGAPORE SLING
DRINK RECIPE 45

remains—a spectacular mahogany bar. Built by Brunswick, the pool table manufacturer, it traveled by ship fully assembled around Cape Horn. Originally fifty feet long—it now measures a still impressive forty-six feet—the bar features a pavilionlike structure capped with a bronze dome. Set at an angle and slightly elevated from the rest of the bar, this area originally served as the cashier's desk from which the attendant could see the entire room.

Although today's barroom is situated in its original location, the bar itself has been moved and modified over the years, cut in half at one point, then restored to its original configuration. In 1936, manager Stephen Royce proposed an update of the room, noting in a memo that, "It is the only place of its kind in the vicinity of San Diego, and if improved and renovated, this feature of the hotel will be brought up to the standard expected at Hotel Del Coronado and the revenue from the buffet supper dances and bar will be, without doubt, greatly increased." During World War II, the bar was a haven for military personnel, a num-

ber of whom were billeted at the hotel. For many, a cocktail at The Del with a pretty girl was the last bright moment in their lives.

The bar has gone by various names over the years: Terrace Bar, Casino Lounge, Oceanview Room, Ocean Terrace, and since 2001, Babcock & Story, in honor of The Del's founders. Unlike some resort hotel bars, which assume the dark, masculine look common to urban hotels, Babcock & Story is a bright place; its wooden ceiling and walls are painted white and the seats are wicker lounges rather than club chairs. During the day, sunshine streams through its many windows, and at night, period ceiling fixtures and floor lamps supply a glow that bounces off the dark wood and mirrored back of the mammoth bar.

In its casual elegance, Babcock & Story distills that unmistakable sense of well-being peculiar to a fine resort. And you don't have to be a guest to feel that sand-between-your-toes, room-by-the sea satisfaction. Even if you've just popped in from a day in one of San Diego's office towers, the sense of escape is palpable.

FOR DECADES, THE DEL HAS OFFERED GUESTS SUN, SURF AND GOOD TIMES. THE HOTEL'S BAR-SEEN HERE IN EARLIER INCARNATIONS-HAS LONG BEEN ONE OF THE PROPERTY'S PRIME AMENITIES.

NOTHING MUCH HAS CHANGED IN THE TONGA ROOM-AND THE OLD REGULARS WOULDN'T HAVE IT ANY OTHER WAY.
LOVERS OF KITSCH LIKE IT THAT WAY, TOO.

THE FAIRMONT SAN FRANCISCO

The term "classic" is very elastic. After all, a classic martini calls for gin and at least some vermouth. However, nowadays, most martinis are made with vodka and vermouth never comes near them. When it comes to hotel bars, "classic" is equally elastic. The standard is a masculine-looking preserve with dark wood, white-jacketed waiters, and heavy silver dishes of almonds at every table. Although surely classic, the Tonga Room of the Fairmont San Francisco broke that mold years ago. Its faux South Seas decor may seem dated even to lovers of the fashionably retro, but the bar endures, a testament to one of those times when Americans got a taste for the exotic, even if it was ersatz.

The Fairmont was built atop San Francisco's Nob Hill in 1906. A Beaux Arts palace, it rose above the district like a Greek temple. But just days before its scheduled inauguration, the earth shook, and within twenty-four hours, flames had reduced the neighboring mansions to smoldering ruins. The Fairmont still stood, but its interior was destroyed. Author Gertrude Atherton, who witnessed the destruction from a distance, described "a tremendous volume of white smoke pouring from the roof, every window a shimmering sheet of gold . . . The Fairmont will never be as demonic in its beauty again." Determined to restore the hotel, owners Herbert and Hartland Law hoped to engage architect Stanford White. Before they could proceed, he was killed by multimillionaire Harry K. Thaw, with whose wife White had had an affair. The brothers turned instead to Julia Morgan, who would later spend twenty-eight years creating William Randolph Hearst's castle compound at San Simeon. The hotel opened on April 18, 1907.

The Tonga Room didn't debut until 1945 when owner Benjamin Swig determined that the area devoted to the hotel's indoor pool—known as the Fairmont Plunge—could be better utilized as a barroom. Inspired perhaps, by the success of Jules "Trader Vic" Bergeron, who had opened his first Polynesian-style restaurant across the Bay in Oakland back in the 1930s, Swig went to work.

For the floor of his new nightspot, he acquired timber that had served as the deck for the SS *Forrester,* a vessel that had sailed the seas from San Francisco. The pool itself became a lagoon where a canopied boat still floats back and forth bearing a band playing Top 40 music. As guests sip Mai Tais under thatched roofs, intermittent lightning and thunder and an occasional downpour punctuate their conversations. A trip to the Tonga Room isn't for everyone. But then again, neither is a carriage ride in Central Park, a visit to the La Brea Tar Pits, or an evening listening to Don Ho in Honolulu. The choice is yours.

THE FAIRMONT SAN FRANCISCO
950 MASON STREET
SAN FRANCISCO, CALIFORNIA
415.772.5000

THE TONGA ROOM MAI TAI (SIGNATURE DRINK)
DRINK RECIPE 46

THE MARK HOPKINS
INTER-CONTINENTAL HOTEL

San Franciscans love the Top of the Mark. "I grew up here," relates bartender David Major, "and my mother, every time she had out-of-town guests, she would always take them to the Top of the Mark." Out of towners love it, too. Along with the Golden Gate Bridge, Lombard Street, and Fisherman's Wharf, countless visitors to the city by the bay rank it one of the town's defining attractions. The crown jewel of the Mark Hopkins Inter-Continental Hotel, the Top of the Mark is one of those attractive rooms in which it is impossible to imagine you're anywhere but where you are.

Although firmly established in the affections of so many, the bar itself is not original to the hotel. The property opened in 1926, named after the cofounder of the Central Pacific Railroad whose many-gabled mansion once stood on the Nob Hill site. The Top of the Mark made its debut in 1939, when owner George D. Smith converted the eleven-room penthouse into a glass-walled cocktail lounge. According to the late *San Francisco Chronicle* columnist Herb Caen, the room got its name by *not* getting a name. Apparently, Smith had told his friends, "I don't know what to call the top of the Mark." "That's it," one of them replied. "Top of the Mark."

Throughout World War II, the Top of the Mark was a popular last stop for Pacific-bound servicemen. Many kept a bottle behind the bar, a "squadron bottle" from which they'd take a drink when safely back in port. Spouses and girlfriends often gathered in the northwest corner of the room to watch the ships depart with their beloved aboard. So regular were their tears that the spot became known as Weepers' Corner.

With the passing of that great generation, few vets come calling, but Major, who has worked the bar since 1985, says that memories of what the Mark meant to those men dies hard. "There used to be a couple of guys who'd come in and order two drinks, one for themselves and one for their dad who'd passed away. One individual's father—a World War II vet—had brought him up here for his first drink when he turned twenty-one. So on the anniversary of his father's death, he'd come up, order his two drinks, and think about his dad."

THE MARK HOPKINS INTER-CONTINENTAL HOTEL
ONE NOB HILL
SAN FRANCISCO, CALIFORNIA
415.392.3434

THE TOP OF THE MARK (SIGNATURE DRINK)
DRINK RECIPE 47

PURPLE HOOTER
DRINK RECIPE 48

ELECTRIC LEMONADE
DRINK RECIPE 49

A POPULAR TOURIST DESTINATION, THE TOP OF THE MARK IS ALSO BELOVED BY SAN FRANCISCANS. STUNNINGLY STREAMLINED IN THE PAST (ABOVE RIGHT), IT HAS RECENTLY ASSUMED A SOFTER, WARMER LOOK (ABOVE LEFT).

THE WESTIN ST. FRANCIS

Everything old is new again when it comes to the Compass Rose Bar of the Westin St. Francis. When the hotel opened in 1904, this rather grand space was known as the Café and served breakfast, lunch, and dinner. The hotel withstood the great quake of 1906, but the fire that followed was brutal. Nonetheless, the St. Francis reopened in 1907 and the Café was back in business.

In 1913, the addition of 4,000 books turned the Café into a lounge area for reading and letter writing. Years after, in an unwonted burst of interest, co-owner, Tempelton Crocker—who had let others play hotelier while he sailed his yacht—decided the St. Francis needed a proper cocktail lounge in the style of the day. So, in 1939, he brought in Tim Pfleuger who had designed the Top of the Mark. Jettisoning every escritoire and settee, Pfleuger utterly transformed the room, installing a Lucite ceiling, black patent-leather walls, and a serpentine bar. Photographs—by none other than Ansel Adams—show the room to be fabulously chic and almost sinful in its sensuous play of materials. While the cognoscenti certainly embraced this modern sanctum, the more conservative crowd took to calling it 'Bar Sinister,' 'The Black Hole,' or 'Coffin Corner.' Although Crocker had dubbed the room the Patent Leather Bar, once he set sail again, management soon renamed it the Orchid Room in an effort to counterbalance the bar's darkly stylish décor.

By 1953, the space had been converted once again and renamed the Terrace Room, with a waitstaff garbed in kimonos. In 1979, the space was spruced up once more, redecorated to recall its initial incarnation. Artisans were brought in to restore the walls, ceilings, and pillars to their original beauty. The windows facing Union Square, hidden since the 1939 redesign, were uncovered. In 1980, the room was rechristened the Compass Rose Bar. The name is taken from the design that appears on the face of compasses and conjures the adventure of travel and a sense of exoticism appropriate to a hotel on the Pacific. Romance and mystery are underscored by the bar's rich trove of appointments, which includes a sixteenth-century Buddhist prayer screen from Burma; nineteenth-century accessories from Japan, Turkey, and Morocco; furniture from China, Korea, Thailand, England, and Italy; and contemporary art from France and Mexico.

THE WESTIN ST. FRANCIS
UNION SQUARE
335 POWELL STREET
SAN FRANCISCO, CALIFORNIA
415.397.7000

COMPASS ROSE WHITE PEACH MARTINI
(SIGNATURE DRINK)
DRINK RECIPE 50

THE SPACE OCCUPIED BY THE COMPASS ROSE BAR (OPPOSITE PAGE) BEGAN LIFE AS THE CAFÉ IN 1904 (ABOVE LEFT).
IT WAS DRAMATICALLY UPDATED IN 1939 (PREVIOUS PAGE) AND AGAIN IN THE 1950S (ABOVE RIGHT) BEFORE ASSUMING
THE OVERSTUFFED ELEGANCE IT POSSESSES TODAY.

THE SORRENTO HOTEL

For all Seattle's relative youth—founded in 1851 and incorporated in 1869—and its identification with information technologies, Starbucks, and grunge music, it has its mature side. And one of the most grown-up places in town is the Sorrento Hotel.

Located on First Hill, an old residential neighborhood within walking distance of such landmarks as Pike Place Market, the Sorrento opened in 1909. The hotel was designed by Harlan Thomas, a Midwesterner who had settled in Seattle a few years prior. From the 1920s through the 1950s, locals and out-of-towners alike enjoyed the Top of the Town—Seattle's first rooftop restaurant, where live entertainment and prime rib were the house specials.

At 150 rooms, the Sorrento was far smaller than most of the great hotels in the country; when Philadelphia's Bellevue-Stratford Hotel opened in 1904, it boasted 1,000 guest rooms. In 1981, new owners decreased the Sorrento's capacity even more, making the property a seventy-six-room hotel. But this reduction did nothing to diminish its appeal; if anything, it distilled its charms to greater potency. The Sorrento is so alluring that countless suitors have chosen it as the place to pop the question. While some fellows drop to their knees in the dining room, others tender their pleas in the Hunt Club Bar or the adjacent Fireside Room. "The guys are always rather nervous," laughs bartender Mark Murphy, who has been asked to garnish at least one martini with a diamond ring.

"But I've never seen anyone turned down and I've seen just jubilation from the women."

With all that wooing going on, one might expect the Sorrento to be one of those painfully trendy hotels that cater exclusively to the young and fashionable. But plenty of well-established folks find their way here, many of them on a regular basis. "We have the old money on house accounts," notes Murphy. "We know exactly what they like and where they like to sit." Classic cocktails have never gone out of style at the Sorrento, and Murphy has mixed up many a Rob Roy, Old Fashioned, Grasshopper, and Pink Lady. "These folks know what they like," says Murphy, "and if you don't make their drink properly, they'll tell you right away."

THE SORRENTO HOTEL
900 MADISON STREET
SEATTLE, WASHINGTON
206.622.6400

THE GRASSHOPPER
DRINK RECIPE 51

THE DRINK
RECIPES

THE BOSTON RITZ FIZZ | RECIPE 4

HOTEL BARTENDERS HAVE BEEN
CONCOCTING DRINKS FOR A LONG
LONG TIME. THE FOLLOWING
RECIPES ARE JUST A SAMPLING OF
THE COCKTAILS THAT ARE BEING
POURED IN GREAT AMERICAN
HOTELS THESE DAYS. WHETHER
TRIED AND TRUE OR UTTERLY NEW,
THESE DRINKS SHARE A COMMON
PURPOSE: TO MAKE ONE FEEL
BETTER FOR HAVING PAUSED TO
ENJOY THEM.

(EACH OF THESE RECIPES REPRESENTS A SINGLE SERVING, BUT BE FOREWARNED: SOME
HOTEL BARS POUR A VERY GENEROUS DRINK.)

RECIPE 1	THE ICE BLUE MARTINI	THE BOSTON RITZ FIZZ	RECIPE 4
THE FAIRMONT COPLEY PLAZA **THE OAK BAR** **BOSTON, MASS**	(signature drink) ½ ounce blue curaçao 6 ounces citrus-flavored vodka, preferably Smirnoff's Lemon twist Put curaçao and vodka in a cocktail shaker with plenty of cracked ice. Shake well and strain into a chilled cocktail glass. Garnish with the lemon twist.	(signature drink) ½ ounce blue curaçao 1 ounce amaretto ½ ounce sour mix Chilled Brut champagne Lemon twist Put the curaçao, amaretto, and sour mix in a mixing glass with plenty of cracked ice. Shake well and strain into a chilled champagne flute. Top with the champagne and garnish with the lemon twist.	**THE RITZ-CARLTON, BOSTON** **THE BAR** **BOSTON, MASS** PHOTOGRAPH ON PAGE 104

RECIPE 2	OAK BAR SIDECAR	MATILDA	RECIPE 5
THE FAIRMONT COPLEY PLAZA **THE OAK BAR** **BOSTON, MASS**	1½ ounces Cointreau 3½ ounces cognac, preferably Rémy Martin VSOP 2 ounces sour mix Sugar Put Cointreau, cognac, and sour mix in a cocktail shaker with plenty of cracked ice. Shake well and strain into a chilled, sugar-rimmed cocktail glass.	2 ounces mandarin-flavored vodka, preferably Absolut Splash of Triple Sec Juice of 1 orange ½ ounce chilled Moët & Chandon Champagne Orange twist Put the vodka, Triple Sec, and orange juice in a cocktail shaker with plenty of cracked ice. Shake well and top with the champagne. Strain into a blue-stemmed cocktail glass. Garnish with the orange twist.	**THE ALGONQUIN HOTEL** **NEW YORK, NY**

RECIPE 3	THE BERRIES	VICIOUS CIRCLE	RECIPE 6
THE FAIRMONT COPLEY PLAZA **THE OAK BAR** **BOSTON, MASS** ◀ PHOTOGRAPH ON LEFT	1½ ounces Chambord 2½ ounces raspberry-flavored vodka, preferably Smirnoff's 2½ ounces strawberry-flavored vodka, preferably Smirnoff's Strasberi 6 raspberries soaked in vodka Put the Chambord and flavored vodkas in a cocktail shaker with plenty of cracked ice. Shake well and strain into a chilled cocktail glass. Garnish with the vodka-soaked raspberries.	1¼ ounces Grand Marnier ¾ ounce rum, preferably Mount Gay 2 ounces passion fruit nectar Put the Grand Marnier, rum, and passion fruit nectar in a cocktail shaker with plenty of cracked ice. Shake well and strain into a chilled cocktail glass.	**THE ALGONQUIN HOTEL** **NEW YORK, NY**

RECIPE 7

THE CARLYLE

BEMELMANS BAR

NEW YORK, NY

THE OLD CUBAN

(a Champagne Mojito)

6 fresh mint leaves
1 ounce simple syrup (use equal parts
    sugar and water)
¾ ounce lime juice
1 dash Angostura bitters
1½ ounce top-quality rum,
    preferably eight-year-old Bacardi
Chilled champagne
Vanilla bean

Put the mint leaves, simple syrup,
lime juice, and Angostura bitters in
a cocktail shaker. Add the rum and
plenty of cracked ice. Shake well and
strain into a chilled cocktail glass.
Top with the champagne and garnish
with three-quarters of the vanilla
bean (a whole bean will be too long).

PHOTOGRAPH ON RIGHT ▶

LONG ISLAND ICED TEA

½ ounce vodka
½ ounce tequila
½ ounce gin
½ ounce light rum
½ ounce Triple Sec
½ ounce sour mix
¼ ounce diet cola
Lemon wedge

Add all the ingredients except the
cola and lemon garnish one at a time
to a highball glass filled with ice. Do
not mix to combine; the drink should
look layered. Add diet cola and garnish with the lemon wedge.

RECIPE 9

THE PLAZA HOTEL

THE OAK BAR

NEW YORK, NY

RECIPE 8

THE PLAZA HOTEL

THE OAK BAR

NEW YORK, NY

OLD FASHIONED

1 cube sugar
Dash of bitters
1 Maraschino cherry
2 ounces blended whiskey
Dash of club soda
Orange wedge

Dip the sugar cube in the bitters
and put it in an old-fashioned glass.
Add the cherries and orange slices
and, using a muddler, crush the fruit
and sugar together. Add the blended
whiskey, then fill the glass with ice.
Top with a dash of club soda.
Garnish with the orange wedge.

BRONX COCKTAIL

½ ounce gin
½ ounce dry vermouth
½ ounce sweet vermouth
Juice of ¼ orange
Orange slice

Combine all the ingredients except
the orange garnish in a cocktail shaker
with plenty of cracked ice. Shake well
and strain into a chilled cocktail glass.
Garnish with the orange slice.

RECIPE 10

THE PLAZA HOTEL

THE OAK BAR

NEW YORK, NY

THE RED SNAPPER | RECIPE 11

RECIPE 11

THE ST. REGIS
HOTEL

THE KING COLE BAR
AND LOUNGE

NEW YORK, NY

THE RED SNAPPER

(a.k.a. Bloody Mary)

2 ounces tomato juice
2 dashes of salt
2 dashes of black pepper
2 dashes of cayenne pepper
3 dashes of Worcestershire sauce
1 dash of lemon juice
1½ ounces vodka
Lemon wedge
Thick celery stick, leaves on

Put the tomato juice, salt, pepper, cayenne, Worcestershire sauce, and lemon juice in mixing glass. Stir to combine. Pack a highball- or wineglass with ice, then add the vodka and the Red Snapper mixture. Garnish with the lemon wedge and celery stick.

◀ PHOTOGRAPH ON LEFT

RECIPE 12

THE PARK HYATT
PHILADELPHIA AT
THE BELLEVUE

LIBRARY LOUNGE

PHILADELPHIA, PA

THE CLOVER CLUB

2 ounces gin
1 ounce lime or lemon juice
2 teaspoons raspberry syrup
1 or 2 dashes of Peychaud's bitters
1 egg white, or 1 tablespoon
    pasteurized egg white
Lime slice

Put the gin, lime juice, raspberry syrup, bitters, and egg white in a cocktail shaker with plenty of cracked ice. Shake vigorously for one minute then strain into a chilled cocktail glass or wine goblet. Garnish with the lime slice.

CONTINENTAL BAR MANHATTAN

3 ounces Wild Turkey bourbon
½ ounce sweet vermouth
½ ounce dry vermouth
Lemon twist

Put the Wild Turkey and both kinds of vermouth in a cocktail shaker with plenty of cracked ice. Shake well and strain into a tumbler filled with ice. Garnish with the lemon twist.

MAYFLOWER ROYAL

(signature drink)

3 ounces vodka, preferably Belvedere
Dash of dry vermouth
¼ ounce Chambord
Lemon twist

Put the vodka and vermouth in a mixing glass and stir to combine. Pour into a chilled cocktail glass. Top with the Chambord and garnish with the lemon twist.

TOWN & COUNTRY

(signature drink)

1¼ ounces vodka, preferably Absolut
1 ounce Midori
3 ounces pineapple juice
¼ ounce Chambord
Lime wedge

Put the vodka, Midori, and pineapple juice in a mixing glass and stir to combine. Pour into a chilled cocktail glass. Top with the Chambord and garnish with the lime wedge.

RECIPE 13

OMNI WILLIAM PENN
HOTEL

THE TAP ROOM

PITTSBURGH, PA

RECIPE 14

RENAISSANCE
MAYFLOWER HOTEL

TOWN & COUNTRY
LOUNGE

WASHINGTON, D.C.

RECIPE 15

RENAISSANCE
MAYFLOWER HOTEL

TOWN & COUNTRY
LOUNGE

WASHINGTON, D.C.

HENRY CLAY'S SOUTHERN-STYLE MINT JULEP

THE WILLARD
INTER-CONTINENTAL
WASHINGTON

THE ROUND ROBIN
BAR

WASHINGTON, D.C.

(signature drink)

6 to 8 fresh mint leaves, plus 1 sprig
    for garnish
1 tablespoon sugar
2 ounces Bourbon, preferably
    Maker's Mark
1 ounce sparkling water
Lemon twist
Superfine sugar

Put the mint leaves, sugar, and one ounce bourbon in a tumbler. Gently muddle with a spoon. Add a scoop of cracked ice and stir vigorously. Top off with more cracked ice. Add equal measures of bourbon and sparkling water to fill glass. Garnish with the fresh mint sprig and lemon twist; dust with the superfine sugar.

PHOTOGRAPH ON RIGHT ▶

THE RHODODENDRON

RECIPE 18

THE GREENBRIER

THE OLD WHITE
LOUNGE

WHITE SULPHUR
SPRINGS, WV

(signature drink)

1½ ounces rum, preferably Bacardi
¾ ounce crème d'almond
Juice of ½ lemon
Juice of ½ lime

Put rum, crème d'almond, and lemon and lime juices in a cocktail shaker with plenty of cracked ice. Shake well and strain into a chilled cocktail glass.

RECIPE 17

THE GREENBRIER

THE OLD WHITE
LOUNGE

WHITE SULPHUR
SPRINGS, WV

THE SCARLETT O'HARA

(signature drink)

1½ ounces Southern Comfort
    or other bourbon
¾ ounces cranberry juice
Juice of ¼ lime

Put bourbon, cranberry juice, and lime juice in a cocktail shaker with plenty of cracked ice. Shake well and strain into a chilled cocktail glass.

CARIBBEAN-SPICED BLACKBERRY COCKTAIL

1½ ounces rum, preferably Captain
    Morgan Spiced Rum
¼ ounce blackberry brandy
2 ounces pineapple juice
Three blackberries on a skewer

Put rum, brandy, and pineapple juice in a cocktail shaker with plenty of cracked ice. Shake well and strain into a highball glass with ice. Garnish with the skewered blackberries balanced on the lip of the glass.

HENRY CLAY'S SOUTHERN-STYLE MINT JULEP | *RECIPE 16*

THE EMERALD MARTINI | RECIPE 20

THE EMERALD MARTINI

1¾ ounce vodka, preferably
   Finlandia
¾ ounce Midori
Splash of pineapple juice

Put all the ingredients in a cocktail
shaker over plenty of cracked ice.
Shake well and strain into a chilled
cocktail glass. Serve straight up.

SEELBACH COCKTAIL

1½ ounces bourbon
½ ounce Triple Sec
7 dashes of Peychaud's bitters
7 dashes of Angostura bitters
4 ounces chilled champagne
Orange twist

Put the bourbon, bitters, and Triple
Sec in a mixing glass and stir to
combine. Pour into a champagne
flute. Top with the champagne and
garnish with the orange twist.

THE SAZERAC COCKTAIL

(signature drink)

1 sugar cube
3 dashes of Peychaud's bitters
1½ ounces rye whiskey or
   bourbon, preferably 18-year-old
   Sazerac Rye Whiskey or Buffalo
   Trace Bourbon
¼ ounce Herbsaint
Lemon twist

Pack an old-fashioned glass with
cracked ice. Put the sugar cube and
bitters in a second old-fashioned
glass. Crush the sugar cube with a
muddler and add the whiskey. Empty
the ice from the first glass and coat
the chilled glass with the Herbsaint,
discarding the extra liqueur. Add the
sweetened bitters and whiskey mixture. Garnish with the lemon twist.

THE VIEUX CARRÉ COCKTAIL

(signature drink)

1 ounce rye whiskey
1 ounce Cognac
1 ounce dry vermouth
½ teaspoon Benedictine DOM
Dash of Peychaud's bitters
Dash of Angostura bitters
Lemon twist

Put the whiskey, Cognac, Benedictine,
and both kinds of bitters in a cocktail
shaker with plenty of cracked ice.
Shake well and strain into a large old-
fashioned glass filled with ice.
Garnish with the lemon twist.

BULL SHOT

2 ounces vodka
4 ounces beef consommé
1 teaspoon lemon juice
1 to 2 dashes of Worcestershire sauce,
   to taste
1 to 2 dashes of Tabasco Sauce,
   to taste
⅛ teaspoon celery salt
1 to 2 dashes freshly ground black
   pepper, to taste

Put the vodka, consommé, lemon
juice, Worcestershire sauce, Tabasco,
celery salt, and pepper in a mixing
glass. Stir to combine. Pour into a
chilled tumbler filled with ice.

RECIPE 25	ORANGE OASIS	APPLE MARTINI	RECIPE 28

THE DRAKE HOTEL

THE COQ D'OR

CHICAGO, IL

ORANGE OASIS

1½ ounces vodka, preferably
   Finlandia
¼ ounce Grand Marnier
Splash of orange juice
Splash of lemon juice
Lemon twist

Put the vodka, Grand Marnier,
orange and lemon juices in a mixing
glass and stir to combine. Pour into a
chilled cocktail glass. Garnish with
the lemon twist.

APPLE MARTINI

3 ounces vodka
2 ounces apple schnapps, preferably
   Apple Pucker
1 ounce Midori
Splash of Southern Comfort
Apple wedge

Put the vodka, schnapps, Midori,
and Southern Comfort in a cocktail
shaker with plenty of cracked ice.
Shake well and strain into a chilled
cocktail glass. Garnish with the
apple wedge.

THE PFISTER HOTE

LOBBY LOUNGE

MILWAUKEE, WI

RECIPE 26	STINGER	FRENCH 75	RECIPE 29

HILTON CINCINNATI
NETHERLAND PLAZA
HOTEL

THE PALM COURT BAR

CINCINNATI, OH

STINGER

1½ ounces Courvoisier VSOP
¾ ounces light crème de menthe,
   preferably Dekuyper

Put the Courvoisier and crème de
menthe in a cocktail shaker with
plenty of cracked ice. Shake well and
strain into a highball glass filled
with ice.

FRENCH 75

¾ ounce cognac
1½ ounces sour mix
1½ ounces superfine sugar
5 ounces chilled champagne
Orange or lemon twist
Maraschino cherry

Put cognac, sour mix, and sugar in
a cocktail shaker with plenty of
cracked ice. Shake well and strain
into a champagne flute. Top with the
champagne and garnish with the
orange or lemon twist and the cherry.

THE PFISTER HOTE

LOBBY LOUNGE

MILWAUKEE, WI

PHOTOGRAPH ON RIGHT

RECIPE 27	CAFÉ NETHERLAND	THE BILTMORE COSMOPOLITAN	RECIPE 30

HILTON CINCINNATI
NETHERLAND PLAZA
HOTEL

THE PALM COURT BAR

CINCINNATI, OH

CAFÉ NETHERLAND

1¼ ounces Kahlúa
1¼ ounces Bailey's Irish Cream
1¼ ounces Frangelico
Hot coffee
Whipped cream (optional)

Put the Kahlúa, Bailey's Irish Cream,
and Frangelico in a large wineglass.
Top with the coffee. Add whipped
cream, if desired.

THE BILTMORE COSMOPOLITAN

(signature drink)

2 ounces citrus-flavored vodka,
   preferably Ketel One Citron
½ ounce Triple Sec
1 ounce cranberry juice
Splash of lime juice
Lime twist

Put the vodka, Triple Sec, and cranberry juice in a cocktail shaker with
plenty of cracked ice. Shake well, add
the lime juice, and strain into a
chilled cocktail glass. Garnish with
the lime twist.

THE ARIZONA
BILTMORE

SQUAW PEAK LOUNG

PHOENIX, AZ

RECIPE 31 — ASPEN CRUD

(signature drink)

5⅓ scoops French vanilla ice
    cream, preferably Häagen-Dazs
3 ounces bourbon, preferably
    Jack Daniels
Milk, if necessary

Put ice cream in a blender and add the bourbon. Blend for several seconds to the consistency of a rich milkshake. If drink is too thick, add milk sparingly and blend again. Pour into a highball glass and serve with a spoon.

NEGRONI — RECIPE 34

1 ounce premium gin, preferably
    Beefeater or Bombay
1 ounce Campari
1 ounce sweet vermouth
Lemon twist

Put the gin, Campari, and vermouth in a pint glass with plenty of cracked ice. Stir well and strain into a chilled cocktail glass. Garnish with the lemon twist.

RECIPE 32 — TAVERN COFFEE

1¼ ounces Bailey's Irish Cream
1¼ ounces Chambord, plus more
    for drizzling
6 ounces hot coffee
Whipped cream

Warm a stemmed glass by running it under hot water. Add the Bailey's, Chambord, and coffee. Stir to combine. Top with the whipped cream and drizzle with additional Chambord.

ROB ROY — RECIPE 35

1¾ ounces premium scotch
½ ounce sweet vermouth
Maraschino cherry

Put the scotch and vermouth in a pint glass with plenty of cracked ice. Stir well and strain into a chilled cocktail glass. Garnish with the cherry.

RECIPE 33 — BACARDI COCKTAIL

4 sugar cubes
Juice of 1½ lemons, strained
    of seeds
1¼ ounces Bacardi rum
Splash of grenadine
Orange twist
Maraschino cherry

Put sugar cubes and lemon juice in a pint glass and crush the cubes with a muddler. Fill with plenty of crushed ice and add rum and grenadine. Shake well and strain into a brandy snifter. Garnish with the orange twist and cherry.

7TH STREET COSMO BLANCO — RECIPE 36

(signature drink)

1½ ounces Absolut Kurant
1½ ounces white cranberry juice
Splash of Chambord
Three blackberries on a skewer

Put the vodka, cranberry juice, and the Chambord in a cocktail shaker with plenty of cracked ice. Shake well and strain into a chilled cocktail glass. Garnish with the skewered blackberries.

RECIPE 37	ADOLPHUS SIDECAR	THE MENGER MARGARITA	RECIPE 39

RECIPE 37

THE HOTEL
ADOLPHUS

DALLAS, TX

ADOLPHUS SIDECAR

(signature drink)

1½ ounces cognac, preferably Rémy
    Martin VSOP
¾ ounce Cointreau
Sugar
Splash of lime juice

Put the cognac and Cointreau in a
cocktail shaker with plenty of cracked
ice. Shake well and strain into a
chilled, sugar-rimmed cocktail glass.
Add the splash of lime juice.

THE MENGER MARGARITA

(signature drink)

1½ ounces of tequila, preferably
    Jose Cuervo
1⅛ ounces of Triple Sec
2 splashes of Rose's lime juice
1⅛ ounces of fresh orange juice
Sour mix to taste
Salt
Lime wedge

Put the tequila, Triple Sec, lime juice,
orange juice, and sour mix in a cocktail shaker with plenty of cracked ice.
Shake well and strain into a salt-
rimmed cocktail glass. Garnish with
the lime wedge.

RECIPE 39

THE MENGER
HOTEL

SAN ANTONIO, TX

PHOTOGRAPH ON RIGHT ▶

RECIPE 38

THE MELROSE
HOTEL

THE LIBRARY BAR

DALLAS, TX

THE LIBRARY MARTINI

(signature drink)

3½ ounces citrus-flavored vodka,
    preferably Absolut Citron
½ ounce Chambord
½ ounce Midori
Orange twist

Put the vodka, Chambord, and
Midori in a cocktail shaker with
plenty of cracked ice. Shake well
and strain into a chilled cocktail
glass. Garnish with the orange twist.

THE WHALER

(signature drink)

1 ounce brandy
1 ounce Kahlúa
1 ounce white crème de cacao
5 scoops premium vanilla ice cream

Comine all the ingredients in a
blender and blend to the consistency
of a thick milkshake. Pour into a
chilled brandy snifter.

RECIPE 40

LA VALENCIA HOTEL

THE WHALING BAR

LA JOLLA, CA

THE BEL-AIR BELLINI

(signature drink)

4 ounces chilled champagne
¾ ounce peach schnapps
Fresh peach slice

Put the champagne and peach
schnapps in a mixing glass and stir
to combine. Pour into a chilled
champagne flute. Garnish with the
peach slice.

RECIPE 41

THE HOTEL BEL-AIR

LOS ANGELES, CA

THE MENGER MARGARITA | *RECIPE 39*

THE PINK PALACE | RECIPE 42

RECIPE 42

THE BEVERLY HILLS
HOTEL

THE POLO LOUNGE

BEVERLY HILLS, CA

◄ PHOTOGRAPH ON LEFT

THE PINK PALACE

(signature drink)

1 ounce gin
½ ounce Grand Marnier
Splash of grenadine
Splash of lemon juice
Lemon twist

Put the gin, Grand Marnier, grenadine, and lemon juice in a cocktail shaker with plenty of cracked ice. Shake well and strain into a chilled cocktail glass. Garnish with the lemon twist.

SINGAPORE SLING

1¼ ounces of gin
2 to 3 ounces sour mix
Splash of club soda
½ ounce of sloe gin
Maraschino cherry
Orange wedge

Put the gin and sour mix in a mixing glass with several ice cubes. Stir well and strain into a chilled Collins glass. Top off with the club soda and sloe gin. Garnish with the cherry and orange wedge.

RECIPE 45

HOTEL
DEL CORONADO

BABCOCK & STORY

SAN DIEGO, CA

RECIPE 43

MILLENNIUM
BILTMORE HOTEL

GALLERY BAR

LOS ANGELES, CA

BLACK DAHLIA

1 ounce Absolut Kurant vodka
1 ounce white crème de cacao
1 ounce Chambord
½ ounce Kahlúa
Maraschino cherry

Put the vodka, crème de cacao, Chambord, and Kahlúa in a cocktail shaker with plenty of cracked ice. Shake well and strain into a chilled martini glass. Garnish with the cherry.

THE TONGA ROOM MAI TAI

(signature drink)

½ teaspoon confectioners' sugar
2 ounces light rum
1 ounce Triple Sec
1 tablespoon almond-flavored syrup
1 tablespoon grenadine
1 tablespoon lime juice
Maraschino cherry
Pineapple wedge

Put sugar, rum, Triple Sec, syrup, grenadine, and lime juice in a cocktail shaker with plenty of cracked ice. Shake well and strain into a large old fashioned glass about one-third full of crushed ice. Garnish with the cherry speared with the pineapple wedge.

RECIPE 46

THE FAIRMONT
SAN FRANCISCO

THE TONGA ROOM

SAN FRANCISCO, CA

RECIPE 44

HOTEL
DEL CORONADO

BABCOCK & STORY

SAN DIEGO, CA

KLONDIKE BAR

1 ounce white crème de menthe
½ ounce Frangelico
½ ounce crème de cacao
Splash of half-and-half
Fresh mint sprig

Put the crème de menthe, Frangelico, crème de cacao, and half-and-half in a cocktail shaker with plenty of cubed ice. Shake well and strain into a chilled martini glass. Garnish with a sprig of mint.

RECIPE 47

THE MARK HOPKINS
INTER-CONTINENTAL
HOTEL

THE TOP OF THE
MARK

SAN FRANCISCO, CA

THE TOP OF THE MARK

(signature drink)

3½ ounces top-quality vodka,
   preferably Ketel One
Splash of dry vermouth, preferably
   Vya
Tomolive (a zesty little pickled green
   tomato)

Put the vodka and vermouth in a
cocktail shaker with plenty of cracked
ice. Shake well and strain into a
chilled cocktail glass. Garnish with
the tomolive.

RECIPE 48

THE MARK HOPKINS
INTER-CONTINENTAL
HOTEL

THE TOP OF THE
MARK

SAN FRANCISCO, CA

PURPLE HOOTER

2 ounces vodka, preferably Ketel One
½ ounce Chambord
1 ounce sour mix
Splash of lime juice

Put the vodka, Chambord, sour mix,
and lime juice in a cocktail shaker
with plenty of ice. Shake well and
strain into a cocktail glass.

RECIPE 49

THE MARK HOPKINS
INTER-CONTINENTAL
HOTEL

THE TOP OF THE
MARK

SAN FRANCISCO, CA

ELECTRIC LEMONADE

1½ ounces citrus-flavored vodka,
   preferably Absolut Citron
½ ounce blue curaçao
1 ounce sour mix
Splash of 7-Up

Put the vodka, curaçao, sour mix,
and 7-Up in a cocktail shaker with
plenty of cracked ice. Shake well
and strain into a cocktail glass.

COMPASS ROSE WHITE PEACH MARTINI

(signature drink)

1 to 2 ounces fresh white peach puree
2 ounces premium vodka, preferably
   Absolut
Drop of peach schnapps
Fresh mint leaves
White peach slice

Put the white peach puree in a cocktail shaker with plenty of cracked ice.
Add the vodka and schnapps. Shake
well and strain into a chilled cocktail
glass. Garnish with a few mint leaves
and the slice of white peach.

THE GRASSHOPPER

1 ounce green crème de menthe
1 ounce white crème de menthe
1 ounce half-and-half

Put both kinds of crème de menthe
and the half-and-half in a cocktail
shaker with plenty of cracked ice.
Shake well and strain into a stemmed
glass.

RECIPE 50

THE WESTIN
ST. FRANCIS

THE COMPASS
ROSE BAR

SAN FRANCISCO, CA

RECIPE 51

THE SORRENTO
HOTEL

HUNT CLUB BAR

SEATTLE, WA

INDEX

DRINKS

Page numbers in *italic* refer to illustrations.

THOMAS CONNORS contributes regularly to the "Good Eating" pages of *The Chicago Tribune*. His articles—on food and drink, architecture and design—have appeared in a number of national publications, including *Bon Appétit, House Beautiful,* and *Town & Country*.

Lifestyle photographer **ERICKA MCCONNELL'S** work has appeared in numerous magazines including *Food & Wine, Martha Stewart Living, Travel + Leisure, Bon Appétit,* and *Life Time,* as well as in many books, including *Yoga Within* and *Perfect Feet: Caring and Pampering* (both Stewart, Tabori & Chang). She lives in New York City.

Stylists **ALEXANDRA AND ELIOT ANGLE** are the founders and co-owners of Aqua Vitae, an event and interior design company based in Los Angeles, and the authors of *Cocktail Parties with a Twist: Drink + Food + Style* (Stewart, Tabori & Chang). The Angles have appeared on the Food Network, E! Style, and Fine Living.

HOTEL PHOTOGRAPHY CREDITS

p. 8 courtesy of The Beverly Hills Hotel, photo of Marlene Dietrich; pp. 16-17 courtesy of The Fairmont Copley Plaza, Boston; p. 19 courtesy of The Ritz-Carlton, Boston; p. 20 courtesy of The Algonquin Hotel; p. 23 courtesy of The Carlyle; p. 25 courtesy of The Plaza Hotel; p. 27 courtesy of The St. Regis Hotel, New York; p. 31 courtesy of The Park Hyatt Philadelphia at The Bellevue; p. 32 courtesy of Omni William Penn Hotel; p. 35 courtesy of Renaissance Mayflower Hotel; p. 36 courtesy of The Willard Inter-Continental Washington; pp. 39-40 courtesy of The Greenbrier; p. 44 (upper left) courtesy of Private Collection, New York; pp. 44-45 courtesy of The Breakers, Palm Beach; p. 47 courtesy of The Seelbach; p. 48 courtesy of The Fairmont New Orleans; p. 51 courtesy of The Hotel Monteleone; pp. 54-55 courtesy of Omni Ambassador East Hotel; p. 56 courtesy of The Drake Hotel, Chicago; p. 58 courtesy of Hilton Netherland Plaza Hotel, photo by Miles J. Wolf; p. 61 courtesy of The Pfister Hotel; pp. 64-65 courtesy of The Arizona Biltmore, photos by Don Scheer (p. 64 right) and Heather Schader (p. 65); p. 66 courtesy of The Hotel Jerome; p. 69 courtesy of The Brown Palace Hotel; p. 70 courtesy of The Oxford Hotel, photo by Gifford Ewing/all rights reserved by Gifford Ewing Photographer; p. 72 courtesy of The Driskill Hotel; p. 75 courtesy of The Hotel Adolphus; p. 75 courtesy of The Melrose Hotel; p. 77 courtesy of The Menger Hotel; pp. 80-81 courtesy of La Valencia Hotel; p. 82 courtesy of The Hotel Bel-Air; p. 85 courtesy of The Beverly Hills Hotel, photos by Erhard Pfeiffer (left) and Jonathan Rouse (right); p. 86 courtesy of Millenium Biltmore Hotel, Los Angeles; pp. 89-91 courtesy of Hotel del Coronado; p. 92 courtesy of The Fairmont San Francisco; p. 95 courtesy of The Mark Hopkins Inter-Continental Hotel; pp. 97-99 courtesy of The Westin St. Francis; p. 100 courtesy of The Sorrento Hotel, photo by Mary E. Nichols.

OTHER CREDITS

Location for bar shots on front cover, back cover, and pp. 3, 4, 6, 12, and 102: Millenium Biltmore Hotel, Los Angeles; Crest, p. 105, reprinted courtesy of The Mark Hopkins Inter-Continental Hotel; F. Schumacher & Co. Interior Design Group, New York fabrics and wallpapers were used for photographs of the following drinks: The Old Cuban, p. 109; The Red Snapper, p. 110; Henry Clay's Southern-style Mint Julep, p. 113; The Pink Palace, p. 122; The Sazerac Cocktail recipe, p. 114, reprinted courtesy of Sazerac Company, Inc.